KW-1771-362

ENJOYING THE OUTDOORS

A PROGRAMME FOR ACTION

SCOTTISH NATURAL HERITAGE

AN SNH POLICY PAPER

OCTOBER 1994

Barcode –

Scottish Natural Heritage Library

16162

Information & Library Services
Scottish Natural Heritage

Location - DI

Class No - 79 (411)

CONTENTS

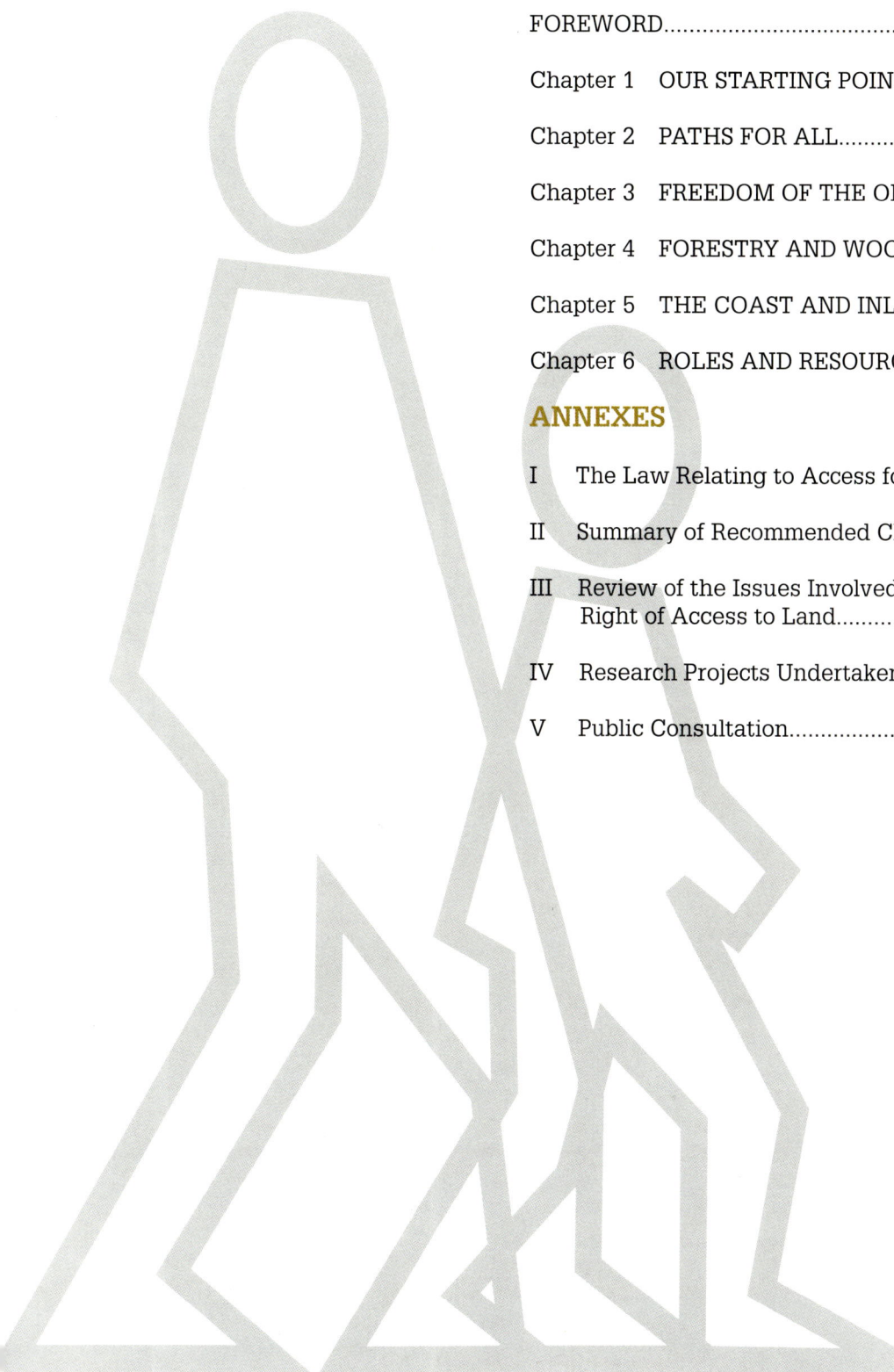

FOREWORD

When Scottish Natural Heritage came into being in April 1992 it inherited from one of its predecessor bodies, the Countryside Commission for Scotland, a major review of the present arrangements for access to the countryside for enjoyment of the outdoors. The Commission had completed a number of research studies; it had consulted many of the key user groups, as well as other organisations and individuals; and it had established a broadly-based Technical Advisory Group to give advice and debate key issues. The main research studies undertaken for the Review (listed in Annex IV) have now been published or are available for inspection.

In taking this Review forward, SNH drew upon these studies and continued the consultation process. In January 1993 we published a discussion paper, *Enjoying the Outdoors*, which invited responses from national and local organisations and local interests and the general public. Some 14,000 copies of this paper were circulated, in order to ensure that the widest possible response was obtained.

This Consultation Paper attracted almost 500 responses, some of them long and closely argued. In January 1994 we published a Summary Report on the responses, prepared (in the interests of objectivity) by Tourism and Rural Initiatives Consultancy Ltd. SNH is grateful to all those who took the time and trouble to set down their views for consideration. The responses provided a very wide range of opinions on possible ways of improving the present situation, and a great deal of useful information about local access issues.

Given the many and varied demands upon the countryside for access, the broad outcome of the consultation was that the present arrangements for recreational access to the countryside are not as satisfactory as they could be and that improvements are now urgently required.

SNH agrees wholeheartedly with this conclusion, and this Paper presents our proposals, and a Programme for Action, for improving access to the countryside.

SNH has, as part of its statutory remit, a duty 'to secure the conservation and enhancement of, and to foster understanding and facilitate the enjoyment of, the natural heritage of Scotland'. It is not our task to make provision for formal recreational activities; it is our responsibility to help to create a framework for responsible access within which people are enabled to achieve a better understanding and a greater appreciation of the beauty and diversity of the Scottish countryside.

SNH's vision is of an accessible and welcoming countryside, but one in which access is arranged so as not to place unreasonable burdens on rural land or on those who live and work in the countryside. Nor should improved access impair the qualities of the natural heritage on which so much of the recreational value of Scotland's outdoors rests. To this end we lay great emphasis on the importance of our five guiding principles of sustainability (see Chapter 1, *Our Starting Point*) to inform any decisions made in this field, and on the role of environmental education in catering for people's growing concern about the protection, the care, the use and the management of the natural heritage.

There are major strategic issues to be tackled. One of the most significant is the question of the 'carrying capacity' of different areas. There are some areas which are ecologically, physically and visually fragile which require remedial measures, perhaps including restrictions on visitors; there are others, such as the lower ground and managed woodland areas, whose carrying capacity is very much greater. We have focused on the development of new access opportunities on the lower ground, especially around settlements close to where most people live: our 'Paths of All' Initiative (see Chapter 2, *Paths for All*) is related to developing further path networks there.

This Paper is a starting point for action and for continued joint working between the key organisations in promoting open-air recreation. It is not a detailed blueprint, because different parts of Scotland require different approaches which can build on the broad policies set out in the Paper.

An encouraging beginning has already been made with the establishment of an Access Forum of the main representative bodies for recreation and landowning, and the relevant public bodies (see Chapter 3, *Freedom of the Open Hill*). Open-air recreation depends on the use of land or water which is mainly in private ownership and often in use for other purposes. Securing accord between those different and sometimes conflicting interests is a challenging task; early success in this endeavour will be a signal of confidence that those who have an interest in, and a commitment to, the enjoyment of Scotland's fine countryside can show each other mutual respect and consideration, to the benefit of all those who love the Scottish countryside.

Magnus Magnusson

Magnus Magnusson KBE
Chairman
Scottish Natural Heritage

SCOTTISH NATURAL HERITAGE'S ROLE IN OPEN-AIR RECREATION

In its founding legislation (the Natural Heritage (Scotland) Act 1991) SNH is charged to facilitate the enjoyment of the natural heritage through inheriting the powers and duties previously held by the Countryside Commission for Scotland under the Countryside (Scotland) Act 1967.

SNH is primarily concerned with informal recreation activities which depend on the qualities of the natural heritage. Sports and physical recreation are the responsibility of the Scottish Sports Council and the agencies involved in promoting tourism also have an involvement in open–air recreation. Other countryside recreations, such as field sports are part of commercial or private land use. Most of these forms of enjoyment touch on SNH's remit in that they use the resources and qualities of the natural heritage which SNH is also charged to conserve and enhance.

There is a critical link between enjoying and conserving the natural heritage. It is in the interests of those who enjoy open-air recreation, and those who benefit economically from recreation and tourism, to care for the natural heritage so that the quality of the places they visit and use (or depend on) is maintained and preferably enhanced. The link between these two themes of conserving and enjoying the natural heritage is strengthened by increasing society's and the individual's understanding of its value. SNH has a key role in this, being charged to promote understanding of the natural heritage, as well as to provide a lead in promoting its sustainable use.

SNH also owns and leases land and manages it as National Nature Reserves. Where it is not limited by the terms of any lease, open access will be available for forms of recreation appropriate to these special places, providing that, as a minimum, their conservation value is not diminished.

Our starting point is that opportunities for enjoyment of the outdoors are of importance to the people of Scotland...open-air recreation contributes to people's health and well-being and thereby benefits society at large.

SNH's vision is of an accessible and welcoming countryside, but one in which access is arranged in ways which do not place unreasonable burdens on rural land or those who live and work in the countryside.

CHAPTER 1

OUR STARTING POINT

This chapter affirms the importance to society of access for open–air recreation, and it sets out the principles on which SNH makes its detailed proposals in the succeeding chapters.

THE IMPORTANCE OF OPEN–AIR RECREATION

Scottish Natural Heritage has a primary responsibility in its founding legislation – the Natural Heritage (Scotland) Act 1991 – to facilitate enjoyment of the natural heritage. This duty stands alongside and equal to SNH's responsibilities for conservation and enhancement of, and for understanding of, the natural heritage.

This report is the first output of a major review by SNH of the arrangements for access to and enjoyment of the countryside for open–air recreation. It sets out an agenda designed to meet the aspirations of society for open–air recreation, to recognise the needs of those who own and manage land and water used by people for their enjoyment, and to allow for the care of the natural heritage.

Our starting point is that opportunities for enjoyment of the outdoors are of high importance to the people of Scotland. Enjoyment of the outdoors provides many people with release from the pressures of modern life and work. Their spirits are refreshed through contact with the natural world and with the

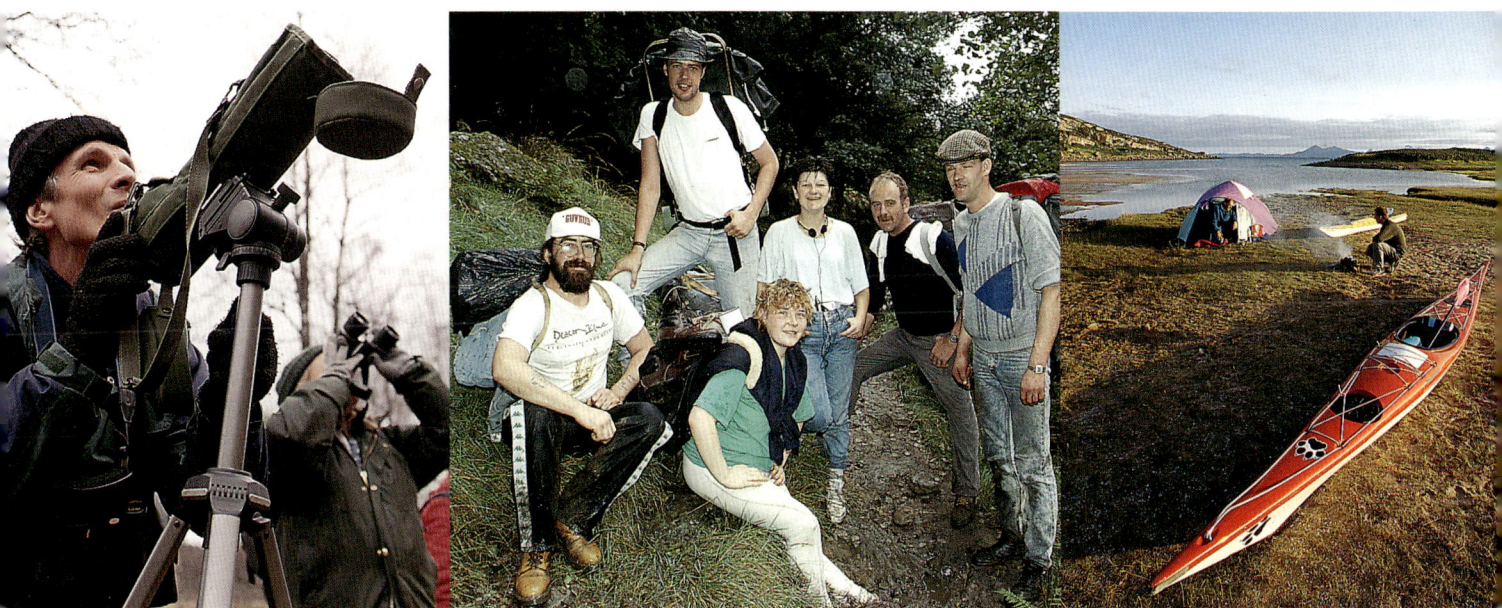

tranquillity of the countryside; great aesthetic pleasure is gained from enjoying fine landscapes or watching wildlife; and increasing numbers of people seek exercise and challenge from participation in active outdoor pursuits. Through all this, open–air recreation contributes to people's health and well–being and thereby benefits society at large.

Scotland is a tourist destination with a strong image – a safe and welcoming country with acclaimed scenery. While there is much to offer the visitor in Scotland's cultural and historic attractions, it is the quality of its countryside which has long attracted people

Scotland is the most attractive part of Britain for some open-air recreations.

There is still insufficient recognition of the high importance of open-air recreation as a key need of modern society.

to holiday here. The rural economy benefits greatly from visitors; indeed tourism is now dominant in the economy of many rural areas, although the land owners and managers who receive visitors on their land seldom share in the financial benefits which come from tourism.

Scotland is the most attractive part of Britain for some open–air recreations. This is especially so for pursuits which use the wilder elements of land or water. Scotland has the bulk of winter snow and ice, the most extensive mountain terrain, a long and very varied coastline, and more inland water space than elsewhere in Britain. Improved roads now make these places all the more accessible and, increasingly, they are valued by visitors from abroad.

The quality of Scotland's outdoors is writ deep in our national culture and pride because the natural heritage is a vital element of the national heritage. The recreational value of Scotland's outdoors depends on the quality of the natural heritage, and this creates a strong bond between enjoyment and conservation. SNH welcomes this as a strength in its work.

–SNH is committed to working for improved access for the enjoyment and understanding of the natural heritage. SNH will promote access in ways which show care and respect for others' interests, which do not devalue the natural heritage and which are sustainable in outcome.

Through an extensive programme of research (listed in Annex IV) and debate, including a major public consultation held during 1993, a wide range of problems on access were identified. The scale of these problems varies greatly around the country but, setting aside the many details, six key themes emerged from the Review which highlight the case for improvements to the present arrangements for access.

1. There is still insufficient recognition of the high importance of open-air recreation as a key need of modern society.

2. The level of planning for, management of and investment in access is too low. Open-air recreation is usually without charge to the user, but management costs arise which are not being adequately funded.

3. The countryside is often not very accessible or welcoming, so that people can find it difficult to know where they can go. Often the network of routes for walking in the countryside is poor, and there is not enough information to help people find places where they can walk freely and feel welcome.

4. Growth in recreation in the countryside affects land management operations and there is evidence of increasing friction. As the range of pursuits widens, with increasing participation, there are more interactions between different forms of recreation, sometimes as they compete for use of the same places.

5. The public are very uncertain about what rights they have to be on land: they are not clear what the law is or whether there is a law relating to trespass.

6. The arrangements in the Countryside (Scotland) Act 1967 for making formal access or footpath agreements have been little used, and new approaches are needed. There is also a consensus that the arrangements for protecting rights of way are too complex and that this contributes to continued loss of these routes.

There is a distinction to be made between access and recreation, access being the means by which people are enabled to participate in all manner of pursuits and pastimes in the countryside, whether by agreement, legal right or tolerance. Clearly the amount and type of recreation which takes place in different areas of the countryside will owe a great deal to the extent of access available, but the effects and needs of recreation should not be confused with the arrangements for access. The availability of access is a pre–condition for recreation which often needs additional planning and management measures. Accessibility refers to the extent to which access can be exercised.

SNH's approach begins with some general principles which apply to all forms of outdoor recreation. Most of this outdoor recreation involves peaceful walking through land which is privately owned and managed for other economic purposes. But increasing numbers of people seek enjoyment through the exhilaration of mechanised and unconstrained forms of recreation, and this can conflict with the enjoyment of others.

Structure of the Report: The rest of Chapter 1 sets out the broad philosophy which underpins SNH's approach to access. Chapters 2 to 5 make proposals for the main settings in which recreation takes place – on land close to settlements, on the open hill, in woodlands and forests, and at the coast or on inland water. Chapter 6 draws together these themes, identifying the roles which different organisations should play in developing better opportunities for access in the Scottish countryside.

A SUSTAINABLE APPROACH TO ACCESS

SNH has a statutory brief to promote a sustainable approach to all activities which affect the natural heritage. We consider that recreation should be treated on the same basis and that enjoyment of the outdoors should always be taken in ways which are sustainable. This should make good sense. The recreational value of the natural heritage is highly dependent on its environmental quality. In turn, the protection of the natural heritage gains strength from the support of those who use it for their enjoyment.

SNH has promoted guidance on sustainable development in a policy paper, *Sustainable Development and the Natural Heritage: The SNH Approach*, published in 1993. SNH's approach is founded upon five main principles. These principles are based on common sense and are designed to promote a sense of responsibility and understanding in how we all use the natural heritage. Enjoyment of the outdoors causes relatively little environmental damage, compared to major land–use impacts, but all the principles – as set out below – have relevance to the access debate.

Outdoor recreation is important for all ages; a learning process for the young, exercise for the elderly.

Wise Use: *Non–renewable resources should be used wisely and sparingly, at a rate which does not restrict the options of future generations.* A major call on non–renewable resources (particularly hydrocarbons) by outdoor recreation activities is the use of the motor car. Use of the car is central to the freedom and flexibility with which people enjoy open-air recreation. But we should aim to be less dependent on the car, especially for the more frequent short and medium length journeys. The provision of better local access, especially where this can be reached on foot or by public transport, will benefit both the environment and the natural heritage and should therefore be a key objective.

Carrying Capacity: *Renewable resources should be used within the limits of their capacity for regeneration.* Many areas of natural vegetation, and some wildlife, are inherently vulnerable to the impact of too much recreation. Scotland lies at northerly latitudes, with harsh winters and cool summers, both of which inhibit quick recovery of damage to natural vegetation on high ground. 'Carrying capacity' refers not just to the physical impacts of people on land, but also to the risk of causing undue disturbance to valued wildlife, and sometimes to the loss of a sense of wildness or solitude – the very qualities which attract people to remote places. The practical implication of this guidance is that there may be a need for restraint on the use of the most vulnerable areas.

Environmental Quality: *The quality of the natural heritage as a whole should be maintained and improved.* Recreation is becoming a major use of land. As outdoor recreation continues to develop, its effects on the natural heritage will become more widespread. There is a need for greater commitment to resolve problems through management, through environmental education, and by strategic planning of the means of access in terms of roads, parking facilities and footpaths.

Precautionary Principle: *In situations of great complexity or uncertainty we should act in a precautionary manner.* Access pressures are sometimes concentrated on places which are ecologically or visually sensitive. Where there is reasonable doubt whether substantial or irreversible damage would be caused to places of special value, the management process should start much earlier, as soon as the problem starts to emerge, and it should seek to identify limits of acceptable change. Meanwhile it is only sensible to constrain and divert activities which might prove damaging to the health of the natural heritage.

Shared Benefits: *There should be an equitable distribution of the costs and benefits (material and non–material) of any development.* We are all 'land–users' in our own ways. Access to the countryside confers great non–material benefits on those who can participate in outdoor recreation. But there can be drawbacks which mainly affect local communities and those who manage land used by the public. Damage now should not compromise the future, either in reducing the enjoyment of generations to come or in creating problems for landowners and managers.

ADDRESSING THE NEEDS OF PEOPLE

The paragraphs above introduce the idea that use of the natural heritage for open–air recreation should be done in ways which are sustainable. This should be matched with concern about the needs of people – both those who participate in open–air recreation and those who own and manage land and water used by others for their enjoyment. SNH identifies three broad principles which underpin its approach to addressing these needs:

Arrangements for access should be equitable: Society places high importance on having good opportunities for open–air recreation and these should be available for all sectors of society. The needs of all sectors, all age groups in society, and the less advantaged, should receive fair attention.

Many people in Scotland – about 40 per cent of all households and more in urban areas – do not have access to their own private transport. Many people have family obligations which inhibit them from full participation in recreation. Others are limited by low income, poor health or disability. SNH wants to encourage more effort to make the countryside more accessible for all.

Another side to equity is that the countryside is a workplace: land managers – be they farmers, foresters, crofters or estate managers – all have to make a living from the land, often in difficult circumstances. For many there are seasonal tasks which have to be accomplished promptly and which can be sensitive to disturbance. For all who earn their livelihood from the land the economic climate is difficult and uncertain. Their task should not be made more difficult and they should receive advice and assistance in the management of access over their land.

There are no simple answers to these difficulties. For some landowners, recreation is not a major problem. For others, the threat or fear of disturbance is in itself a serious worry, especially as there are many fewer people working the land today and able to keep an eye on what is happening there.

On this principle of equity, SNH draws out two main guidelines:

–Everyone should have accessible opportunities for informal and formal recreation pursuits in the countryside. Every effort should be made to cater for the needs of people who are disadvantaged, less able or disabled.

–Where those who own and manage land are suffering significant impact from the public being on their land for open–air recreation, they should be able to seek practical help in the management of these problems.

Access should be based on mutual respect: *SNH's aim is to seek a consensus in arriving at the best arrangements for access.* This will best be achieved by acceptance that access involves responsibilities on all sides – a need for mutual respect. This is required of land owners and managers in responding to society's need for good opportunities for open–air recreation; and there should be better recognition by people visiting land that they have responsibilities to its management and to those who live and work in the countryside. It is SNH's view that we must create a climate for co–operation. This implies a commitment to reach acceptable solutions through consensus where difficulties arise. Our guideline is:

- A co-operative approach to resolving access issues should be based – by land owners and by recreation bodies – on mutual understanding of and responsibility for each others' interests.

Access solutions should be comfortable: *The word 'comfortable' is used in the sense that visitors to land, and land owners and managers, should be able to feel more relaxed about access.* The visitor should be able to feel confident that, when acting with care and following good practice, he or she is welcome. Land owners and managers should be able to feel more confident that visitors are behaving responsibly. They should also be able to expect that there is a shared responsibility through the wider community to help resolve problems. Our guideline, therefore, is that:

- Arrangements for access should promote confidence in visitors about where and when they can be on land, and confidence among land–owners and managers that they will have support when they meet significant problems.

THE ROLE OF THE INDIVIDUAL IN ACCESS

In responses to our Consultation Paper, very many comments were made on the need to promote good behaviour and practice in open–air recreation, especially on the need for more education for understanding. SNH's broad approach is to promote care and respect for the countryside. Our guideline is that:

- Recreational use of land or water should be founded on care, so that those who enjoy the outdoors respect its beauty, its wildlife, its operational needs and the privacy of those who live or earn their living there.

Central to this is a message of restraint and a conscious effort to cause minimum impact. It is about visitors always being thoughtful and considerate when they use other people's land. It is about small–scale and individual actions, such as not climbing walls or fences, not leaving gates open, and not taking dogs onto farms with livestock. It is about showing responsibility in visiting the main stalking estates over the main deer–shooting period. And it is about showing the same courtesy to people who live and work in the countryside as they are expected to show to visitors. It is these simple acts which will help to build mutual confidence: many people show this level of care already, but the message still has to be promoted widely.

These sorts of messages have long been promoted through the Country Code. The Code has survived over many years without substantial change, in part because its messages are still valid and also because its longevity has led to wide use and

Access should be based on mutual respect.

awareness. This should not be lightly set aside. However, many recognise that the Code now needs review, to be refreshed and revised to serve needs in Scotland better. SNH will therefore:

- Take the lead in devising a Country Code for Scotland and in promoting its use; and

- Publish information on the traditions and rights of access and on responsibilities in use of the countryside for recreation.

On the back of the Country Code there has developed an array of other codes, some for the practice of different recreations, others to promote good practice in studying wildlife, or to provide information about access or safety. Codes of this kind are welcomed, although consistent messages should be promoted. SNH will therefore:

- Encourage and assist groups representing sports, recreations and pastimes to prepare and promote codes of good practice for care for the environment and respect for land management needs.

The report of the Government's recent Working Party on Environmental Education - *Learning for Life* - promotes a broad agenda for education about the environment. Environmental education can make a major contribution to promoting good behaviour in and understanding of the countryside by all age groups, in particular the young. Through its work on access, SNH will itself and with others promote messages to the younger generations on understanding land use needs and the environment, and on the need for responsible behaviour when visiting the countryside.

The agenda outlined above is both challenging and important. The general message from the Consultation Paper was that the arrangements for access need improvement. No one responded to say that there was no issue to address, and most agreed that the review was timely and that some change is needed.

SNH considers that the promotion of a responsible approach to public access is vitally important, and the best guarantee in the long term that the natural heritage will be cherished and protected for the use of future generations. It is important that we can agree solutions which respect the broad principles set out above, of being sustainable, equitable, based on mutual respect and comfortable. This approach can help to promote consensus working on the improvement of access for open–air recreation, an outcome of great value to the people of Scotland and to those who visit our country.

DUNCRYNE *is private*
WELL BEHAVED VISITORS ARE
WELCOME TO USE THE TRACK
AND HILLTOP . PLEASE DO NOT
WANDER INTO THE WOODS.
(RESERVED FOR TEDDY BEARS ETC.....)
HELP US BY CLEARING LITTER
LEFT BY LESS TIDY VISITORS
WE HOPE YOU ENJOY SHARING

our point of view.

Local access is the most urgent issue on which to make progress...to create more welcoming and assured access for the visitor to the countryside and to help farmers and other land managers to cope with any problems which may arise.

SNH's vision for local access is that communities throughout Scotland should have good networks of paths which are accessible and welcoming.

CHAPTER 2

PATHS FOR ALL

This chapter sets out SNH's proposals for a 'Paths for All' initiative to improve local access for informal recreation,close to towns and settlements. It also deals with some specific management issues.

Most walks in the countryside are short and taken from home or close to it, or where people are staying on holiday. For those who travel to the countryside for recreation the average journey is also short. Most of these trips are made by car, but some 40 per cent of households in Scotland do not have their own private transport and have difficulty in reaching the countryside. These facts emphasise the importance of local access close to towns and cities as well as in the busy tourist areas. Promoting local access is also important for a more sustainable approach to access, particularly in looking ahead to help reduce the consumption of scarce energy resources, especially by use of the car, a principle set out in Chapter 1.

Much has been done to improve local access in some areas through local authorities' work on rights of way, through the network of Country Parks and through other managed recreation sites close to towns. Countryside Around Towns projects, which aim to improve landscapes blighted in the past and to encourage more access, have also made a contribution. Overall, however, much improvement is still needed to create more welcoming and assured access for the visitor to the countryside.

A number of crucial problems for local access were identified in research for the Review;

in some areas there is a severe shortage of paths and tracks which can be used by the public with confidence;

most paths already in use are not signed and there is little information about where people can go to walk, especially for visitors to an area.

A sign of tension between farmer and visitor.

physical barriers or deterring signs restrict visits to some areas of the countryside, although this often arises where farmers and land managers have concerns about security, about vandalism and sometimes about violence or other criminal behaviour;

–A low profile and low priority have been given at the national and local levels to promote action and to provide funding for local access;and

local authorities have difficulty in using the procedures for protecting rights of way, and this has led to a mainly reactive approach to solving problems and also to many existing paths having uncertain status and poor long–term security against their loss.

The opportunities for walking close to settlements have diminished as the motor car has made rural roads less safe or less pleasant for walking. There is increasing demand for cycling off–road and for horse–riding, as well as for other recreation activities. Yet the arrangements in Scotland for access to countryside close to towns, and especially, through farmland, compare badly with other countries. For example, there is no definitive map of rights of way such as exists south of the Border and as shown on Ordnance Survey maps there; nor can Scotland compare with Germany, where there is a general right of access to tracks and paths in the countryside.

Land close to towns is often under heavy pressure from varied uses, and some farmers have a hard time coping with the impacts which arise. Farming close to settlements can greatly restrict the options available to make best use of the land and farmers often have real anxieties about vandalism and theft. Many of these problems do not come from recreation, being linked to social conditions in adjacent communities; but if there is to be more access on to land close to towns, there must be help for farmers to enable them to feel more comfortable about the public entering their land.

Woodland close to towns, local areas of open land and Regional and Country Parks are all important in providing local access for the wide range of recreations which people want to pursue close to home. However, the greatest local need is for a better network of paths, either for short (and preferably circular) walks, or to gain access to places used for informal recreation – such as viewpoints, local open space, woodland or the water's edge. The main recommendations in this chapter aim to improve opportunities for local access along paths.

–SNH considers that local access is the most urgent issue on which to make progress, and it will establish a national 'Paths for All' initiative in partnership with other key interests.

A 'PATHS FOR ALL' INITIATIVE

–SNH's vision for the development of better local access is simple: within the next decade, communities throughout Scotland should have networks of local paths for the enjoyment of local people and visitors. The 'Paths for All' initiative is about promoting this vision, showing how it can be achieved and assisting the development of local partnerships to make it happen.

The basis for improving local access will be the agreement and promotion of networks of community paths – not just for walkers but also, where appropriate, for cyclists and horse–riders. The word 'network' is taken to mean a system of paths distributed around communities so as to serve local needs; these paths need not always interconnect, but this may be appropriate to create a choice of longer walks or rides.

A local path network will normally be based on existing rights of way, private tracks used for land management, and some still–quiet rural roads. Rights of way alone will usually not be sufficient, or their status perhaps will be unclear (see p.00 below) and additional negotiated paths will be needed. Some of these paths may already exist as permissive paths where use by the public is tolerated. SNH believes that more land owners and farmers would be prepared to open up routes through their land for public use, provided that they could feel confident of support for the resolution of any problems, and that no new rights are created over their land. It will be important that new routes avoid the work centre of the farm staeding and do not impose on farmers' personal privacy.

SNH will promote 'Paths for All' as a national initiative to give a lead to the creation of networks of local paths. This will involve the following actions:

–SNH will set up a 'Paths for All' project team working in collaboration with local authorities and other parties to give a practical lead to the initiative.

–SNH will publish an action guide to assist the development of local community paths and to give stimulus to the whole initiative.

–SNH will offer grant to assist partnership initiatives between communities, local authorities, and land owners and managers to create and promote local networks.

–SNH will encourage each new local authority to appoint a footpath officer, dedicated to promoting path networks and to working on existing rights of way. SNH will be prepared to offer pump priming grant for new posts of this kind on a tapering scale.

–SNH will publish advice on preparing maps of local paths, to encourage all communities to have their own local map readily available.

–SNH will request The Scottish Office to promote legislation to establish a simpler system for the assertion of rights of way, and to issue guidance to the new local authorities on footpaths and rights of way to give impetus and support to this work.

WALKING IN THE COUNTRYSIDE – KEY RESEARCH FACTS

–More than 2 million walks are taken every week in the Scottish countryside or at the coast by Scottish residents. Walks taken by tourist visitors will add significantly to this total.

–The majority of walks are taken by people who do so frequently – 7 per cent of the population walk daily in the countryside or at the coast and the weekly figure is 12 per cent. On a monthly basis, around 30 per cent of the Scottish population will have taken a walk in the countryside or at the coast.

–Half the population only rarely or never take a walk. Groups in society with lower than average levels of participation are those in the older age groups; people who are not in work; and people in unskilled employment groups.

–Most walks are short. About half of all walks fall in the 2–5 miles category; 20 per cent between one and two miles and 7 per cent of walks are claimed to be less than a mile. But almost a quarter of the respondents claim to have walked more than five miles on their most recent outing.

–One–third of walkers had a dog with them on their last walk, rising to 40 per cent for those walking on their own.

–Most walks are taken close to home. Three–fifths of all walks started from home or where the respondent had stopped the night before. For those who travelled a distance to begin their walk, the mean journey distance was 6.5 miles.

–For most walks the main surface used was a footpath (37 per cent) or a track (18 per cent). Twenty–two per cent of walks were mostly on tarmac roads and 7 per cent across fields with no paths. Six per cent were on the beach and 8 per cent over open country without a path.

–Most walks were in lowland countryside. One–fifth were through farmland and one–fifth in woodland. Eleven per cent were at the edge of inland water – river, reservoir or loch – and 23 per cent at the coast. Nine per cent were claimed to be in town or village and 8 per cent in a mountain or moorland setting.

–Most people (two–thirds) did not meet any obstacles and of those who met a difficulty, wet or boggy ground was the most common complaint. Very few people were deterred by obstructions, but most people (85 per cent) were on a route they had been on before.

Source – Survey of Walking by System 3 Scotland. Sample size 4107 in four surveys – April, July, October and January 1990–91

–SNH will, through technical advice, training and research, continue to develop innovative ways of helping with the development of better local access, and it will promote high standards of design and management for path networks.

TARGETS FOR 'PATHS FOR ALL'

SNH wants to promote early action on 'Paths for All'. With local government reform ahead it will be important to start this work soon and to maintain its momentum over the period of change. Key targets for the initiative are:

–The 'Paths for All' initiative to be established in 1995.

–All new local authorities to become partners in the 'Paths for All' initiative.

–Within ten years, properly mapped, promoted and managed networks of local paths to be available for all towns and settlements.

–SNH will publish early in 1995 an Action Guide to assist communities to promote path development.

–SNH will introduce in 1995 a grant scheme in support of the initiative.

–SNH will seek, through The Scottish Office, the early establishment of a representative Working Group to prepare detailed proposals to revise rights of way procedures at the earliest legislative opportunity.

A PARTNERSHIP APPROACH

Action for local access is best delivered through local partnership, led by the local authorities in concert with local communities. There is good work of this kind in different parts of Scotland, for example the 38–mile Dunkeld and Birnam walks system, opened in July 1994. The key is the approach described in Chapter 1 of creating a climate of co-operation and of shared responsibility. This must involve close working with land owners and managers to involve them in developing solutions which recognise their management needs and concerns.

The Dunkeld and Birman walks system.

The key players in partnerships of this kind are:

the local authorities, because only they have the statutory role in local access, the resources, skills and staff to give leadership and assistance to local action;

local communities, represented in various ways, such as the Community Councils, amenity, recreation or other local groups and clubs and individuals, all of whom can contribute local knowledge, enthusiasm and understanding of what is needed locally to improve access;

the farming and landowning communities, whose involvement is crucial because of their ownership of land used by the public; and other relevant local interests such as Local Enterprise Companies and Area Tourist Boards, agricultural advisory services and SNH's own local staff, all of which have a role in helping to fund and support local action.

These interests should be represented in one way or another in the development of local path networks; but the main lead in negotiation and management should come from the local authority working closely with the local community, farmers and land managers.

The general basis of agreeing with the land owners and managers an extended and promoted network of new paths should be that:

new paths (and access to any new areas of open space agreed at the same time) are for informal recreation by foot (or by horse or cycle where agreed) for the purposes of informal enjoyment of the outdoors by individuals and small groups;

the community – using the term in its widest sense of local people, local organisations and councils – will adopt a responsibility to assist in the management and oversight of public use of the network;

land managers should be able temporarily to close a permissive path for stated reasons, or to restrict certain uses, but this should be exercised with restraint;

agreement for new permissive paths should not create any new rights over land;

there should be an agreement in writing between the landowner and the local authority setting down the terms and conditions under which the access has been agreed, but a full statutory footpath creation agreement or a management agreement would normally not be required, except where a large public expenditure (such as for a long footbridge) needs to be safeguarded;

it should be agreed that paths can be promoted by waymarking and local maps or leaflets; and

visitors using the network should be guided by a code of good conduct.

'PATHS FOR ALL' – MAKING IT HAPPEN

In working for better path networks, there are six main factors in getting started and in making effective progress.

Involving all the interests: Getting off to a good start needs the involvement from the outset of all the main interests: a local access group or forum might be one way of bringing together the various parties for discussion. Involving those who own and manage the land is crucial because of their responsibility for its management and stewardship.

Identifying local needs: Identification of the variety of different needs of the local population is crucial. Care is needed to accommodate the needs of those who are older and cannot walk far and need comfortable surfaces to walk on, or parents with a pram and young children, or people who do not have a car, or those who are disabled.

Taking a local overview: Review of people's needs has to be set alongside an overview of the existing supply of routes and the need for additional links to create a useful network. A common sense assessment of the options should be based on discussion with local users and land owners and managers. Taking this overview has value in identifying the broad picture, in providing a vision of what is intended and a framework for the assessment of costs as well as in securing approval and commitment by funding bodies.

Assured and welcoming: Perhaps the most crucial element in improving local access through community paths is to make it assured and welcoming. Information is the key to this, either through maps and leaflets or by invitation on the ground through waymarks, signposts and in some places small car parks.

A mapped approach: All communities should aim to have a map of local routes. Use of a 'Paths for All' logo would help visitors to an area to identify with an information source with which they might already be familiar. SNH will publish advice on the design and preparation of local maps.

Support for the land manager: It is important that farmers and other land managers feel confident that they can get local help to resolve any problems through the community and also from a ranger service which can take a lead in management and maintenance, in promoting care and in mediating on local problems.

GIVING IMPETUS TO 'PATHS FOR ALL'

Creating community path networks is not a simple task: in some areas there is little existing activity or provision, and the forthcoming reorganisation of local government could lead to loss of impetus. To help gain momentum, SNH will discuss with its partners ways of giving a special impetus. Much can be done locally depending upon need, or perhaps upon existing local action. But a more general catalyst is needed and proposes to set up a special project team, in consultation with its key partners, especially with the local authorities. It is not SNH's task to do any of the work locally but to give a lead to 'Paths for All', particularly by the following means.

Advice will be needed on assessing existing local paths, on surveying paths and identifying opportunities for action and priorities; on securing resources, on implementation and on subsequent maintenance and monitoring. Technical advice will be needed on path creation and maintenance, on basic designs for gates and stiles, waymarking and signposts, and on preparing local maps and other packages of information about local walking.

PATHS AND TRACKS: SOME KEY RESEARCH FACTS

There is very little quantitative information about the numbers of paths and tracks, or rights of way available in the countryside for use by the public. A very limited sample survey for eight study areas in the Scottish countryside identified the following facts.

–On average, there is about 1 kilometre length of route per square kilometre of countryside which has the potential to be used by the public (this excludes tracks providing access only to private properties), but the density of these routes varies greatly around different tracts of Scottish countryside. This can be extrapolated to a national figure of 87,000 kilometres of routes with existing or potential recreational use, but this is a very insecure estimate because of the very small size of the survey sample.

–About one–third of this network is already recorded as usable – normally by the local authority – and may have right of way status. The overall network of recorded paths and tracks is significantly less in Scotland than for England and Wales, being only 35 per cent of the average density of rights of way in England and a quarter of the rights of way network in Wales.

–Some 45 per cent of all routes in the survey samples are farm or forest roads, a further 30 per cent are paths of different widths and 23 per cent are lightly trodden routes. Over three–quarters of all routes are shown on the 1:25,000 map.

–Information available on routes varies greatly according to the setting, with some areas having little or no information, while in one tourist area in the sample 70 per cent of routes are promoted.

–Most routes (three–quarters) can be followed easily on the ground and only one–third have some kind of physical obstacle. Five per cent of routes are blocked.

–Only around half of all routes can be used with confidence, the other half having some kind of perceptual deterrent – such as passing close to a private building. Only 3 per cent of routes have notices prohibiting entry. Three–quarters of the routes are in a good or satisfactory condition, and very few are difficult or hazardous. Horse–riding is evident only on 16 per cent of surveyed routes and cycling on 18 per cent of routes. The evidence of horse–riding and cycling varies considerably over the survey areas. Only one of the surveyed routes is recorded as a bridleway.

Source – Field surveys in eight study areas undertaken by Peter Scott Planning Services.

Training for a range of skills is needed for path development, maintenance and promotion, always aiming to secure high standards of design and implementation.

Demonstrations will help lead the way; these could usefully build on existing initiatives.

Promoting communication between all involved in the initiative is vital, using newsletters, seminars, training, and awards or competitions to stimulate action.

Advocacy will be needed both at the local level and also with a wide range of key national organisations and interest groups to secure their involvement, support and goodwill for the initiative.

General promotion of the Initiative, undertaken with key partners, will be important in maintaining a high profile and in helping to give a national context to local action.

FUNDING 'PATHS FOR ALL'

The costs of developing and maintaining path networks should not fall on land owners and managers. These should be met through the relevant public bodies, led by the local authority. SNH will offer grants to assist local communities to create new local paths, the details of which will be announced later. The provision of larger capital items such as car parks or large bridges should continue to be led by the local authority. Grant would also be available to land owners who want to make a contribution to improving access at their own hand by providing or managing access where they are meeting significant impacts from recreation on their land.

There is a need to draw in more resources in addition to SNH's own contribution. Expenditure on local walking has had limited commitment from many authorities in the past, as compared with higher levels of spending on formal recreation facilities. This is disappointing, given the importance of walking for all age groups in the community and for its importance to local tourism. SNH believes that local authorities should now contribute more funds to this work. Local Enterprise Companies are able to finance projects which lead to economic benefits and these bodies have a role to play in supporting local recreation opportunities, especially in the tourist areas.

Government has already made proposals under the Agri–Environment Programme to assist farmers in the Environmentally Sensitive Area schemes (and also for set-aside land generally) to make provision for public enjoyment. SNH considers that there is great potential for creative and sensitive use of agricultural support to assist conservation and also to provide for local access (perhaps along existing tracks) on set–aside land and using field–margins and conservation headlands.

SNH does not believe that it is appropriate to make specific payments through agricultural support schemes where the presence of visitors involves no significant cost to the farmer. Such tolerance should be an accepted benefit to the public arising from agricultural support schemes. SNH does think, however, that

these schemes have a valuable role in contributing to the cost of new access opportunities or where a significant burden from access arises from high levels of public use. Such payments should be directed to those areas of greatest potential or where heavy impacts are already being suffered, so as to achieve the greatest benefit. These 'recreational priority' areas will lie mainly around conurbations and in the busy tourist areas.

Local authorities should be involved, along with the agricultural advisory service, in advising how and where targeting should be done, linking with their ability to undertake their own expenditure (sometimes with grant from SNH). Without collaborative working between all who are involved in access there is a risk of inefficient expenditure. The details of access arranged under agricultural support schemes should always be a matter of agreement with the farmer or land manager.

There is opportunity through the National Lottery or Millennium projects to give a special impetus to 'Paths for All'. SNH will explore how funding from these sources might contribute to the 'Paths for All' initiative.

PUBLIC RIGHTS OF WAY

In the responses to our Consultation Paper, there was comment that SNH appeared to be placing too much emphasis on rights of way as compared with a need to secure access to open country. But rights of way are important: they provide one of the few opportunities whereby the public have at present a clear right to cross land, although this is often a fragile foothold, with most rights of way being unasserted and only having the status of claimed right of way.

The status of right of way is important in protecting access at public inquiries, or in planning for new development or new roads. Also, rights of way are part of the heritage of past use of the countryside. What we have left is a shadow of a former network, part of which has been absorbed into the modern road system. Many rights of way have been lost through lack of use arising from changes in population distribution and from the dominance of travel by car.

Many respondents to the Consultation Paper said that the present arrangements for recording, asserting and managing rights of way were inadequate and need revision if these routes are to have a role in the future as part of an access network. If we cannot improve the systems for recording, asserting and, thereby, promoting rights of way, continued attrition is certain. SNH does not think that local access can be secured solely through rights of way; and they are less relevant in open country. However, more effort to improve local networks close to communities will depend crucially on key routes already in use, many of which will be rights of way.

There is a substantial amount of information available about the problems of rights of way. Two pieces of research were undertaken for the present Paper and the Scottish Rights of Way Society also undertook a review and made proposals for change. The Society has made a valuable contribution to the debate.

The prime need is to make the assertion and recording of rights of way easier. An assessment of the issues for the Review identified that the main technical problems lie in a **lack of certainty** – in other words, full assertion or confirmation of a right of way (sometimes termed 'vindication') requires that the process go through the courts, which is only rarely done. Second, **there is never any finality,** even for the small number of cases taken to law, because the status of an asserted route could be under challenge on expiry of the 20 year prescriptive period.

The prime issue is that the whole process ultimately depends on going through the courts with all the uncertainties and potentially high costs which can arise. Hence the need for a simpler administrative system in which local authorities through their planning function have a more central role in the recording and protection of rights of way. A simpler system should allow for local authorities to review the evidence for the assertion of a right of way and to propose right of way status, subject to the consideration of written objections by an independent reporter. There should be provision for recourse to the courts to remedy any procedural faults by the authorities.

In addition, there is a need to strengthen various minor elements of the law relating to rights of way. Changes for the future care of rights of way should include:

an asserted right of way should be secure until evidence of its non–use over the prescriptive period is presented through the same process of review and objection as is proposed for assertion (variation of rights of way could use the same procedure);

local authorities should have a duty to keep maps showing asserted rights of way and other areas where a right of public access exists, including land where access is agreed as a condition of Capital Tax relief; the present duty on authorities to maintain maps of access agreement areas (Section 26 of the Countryside (Scotland) Act 1967) could be amended for this purpose;

local authorities should have a duty to maintain asserted rights of way but only to a standard appropriate to their location and use; clarification of their powers for maintenance is needed; and

there should be a requirement to signpost asserted rights of way; the erection of misleading signs and deliberately obstructing a right of way should become offences.

SNH's proposals are presented in Annex II and a separate paper on the subject is available. In summary to this section on public rights of way:

–The prime need is that the procedures for assertion of rights of way should be simplified. Legislation is needed to create a new administrative procedure in which the local authorities play a central role in compiling a record of rights of way. This should allow for appeal by other parties using a simplified procedure of written objections reviewed by an independent reporter.

SOME GENERAL ISSUES OF LOCAL ACCESS

There are several broader issues on local access which cannot be handled simply through co-operative work at the local level, such as tackling the more intransigent urban–edge management problems. Some of these issues are considered briefly below. All are of vital importance to improving access generally and all require more effort and commitment, especially by the public authorities.

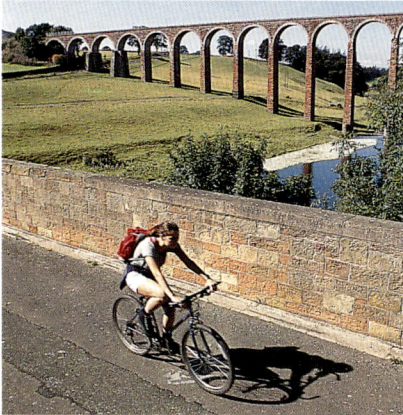

Recreation and transport planning: New approaches to transport planning are emerging which give more emphasis to walking, cycling and public transport. Some Roads Authorities are now adopting policies of this kind in order to provide a more integrated approach to travel, especially in and around towns. The majority of individual leisure journeys are short and a shift of emphasis towards public transport, walking and cycling could add much to the quality of life, help reduce congestion and pollution and promote a more sustainable transport policy, as well as helping people who do not own a car.

–SNH welcomes existing action by some of the present Roads Authorities and encourages the new local authorities to adopt new approaches in their Transport Policies and Programmes which deal more even–handedly with different modes of travel. These should provide for more public transport, walking and cycling, and thereby contribute to better local recreation opportunities. Guidance from Government on this issue is needed.

More emphasis needs to be given to walking, cycling, and public transport.

Getting out of towns: The ability to get out of built–up areas to adjacent countryside often needs action. At the town or city edge, cyclists and walkers may need special help to cross major roads or bypasses. New bypasses for communities are welcome, but they should not be barriers as some are now, which restrict access by people to their local countryside for recreation. The aim should be for separated crossings, either by bridge or underpass, to enable safe passage, especially for the elderly and people with young families who are most easily deterred from crossing busy roads. Motorways, in particular, are major impediments to countryside access on foot, by horse or by cycle.

–SNH calls on the Roads Authorities, and also The Scottish Office as Trunk Roads Authority, to ensure that major road developments do not unnecessarily impede legitimate public access to the local countryside for recreation. Guidance from Government to the Roads Authorities is required.

A countryside management approach: Farmers and other land managers at the edges of large towns and conurbations often face major problems, including chronic vandalism and dumping of litter, and the environment in these places is often degraded from past industrial uses. Several Countryside around Towns projects have addressed these problems and they have succeeded in programmes of work to improve landscape and habitats and to provide recreation. Much depends on the local community having a sense of 'ownership' of schemes to improve their local environment. This type of integrated countryside management should be pursued where management needs are greatest, not

Well located parking is crucial.

just in the countryside around towns but also in the busy tourist areas. Countryside ranger services have a crucial role in helping to deliver an integrated management approach and in helping to mediate on local problems.

Local roadside parking: An undervalued aspect of local access is the ability to pull off the road safely at pleasant places in order to view fine scenery, to have a picnic or to rest on a journey. This is important for people who are unable to participate, even at a modest level, in active forms of recreation, and more could be done to help people enjoy the countryside better in this way. On many rural roads the majority of use is now for recreation through tourist travel. Good design and maintenance of stopping places are important.

Well–located parking is also crucial in making the countryside more accessible for the active pursuits. Often roadside parking for visitors has developed in *an ad* hoc way. Road development has enabled the car to penetrate too far at some locations where a longer walk in could be promoted.

–Off–road parking for informal enjoyment of the countryside is important for people who do not participate in active recreations. Local authorities should ensure that good quality and safe provision is made for off–road parking, through their planning for recreation in the countryside.

DOGS AND ACCESS

Dogs in the countryside – and especially on farmland – provoke strong emotions. Land managers are generally unsympathetic to people bringing dogs when out for recreation. Some visitors can feel threatened by dogs, while others greatly value their companionship and the security they can provide as an important part of their recreation. In the survey of walking (see box on page 20), 30 per cent of respondents said that they had a dog with them on their most recent walk. However, many of the worst problems caused for farmers from dogs are not connected with genuine recreation but come from uncontrolled and unaccompanied dogs.

Views on dogs in responses to the Consultation Paper were wide–ranging and, although some thought that the complaints about dogs were overstated, there was general recognition that there is an issue to address. More control was advocated by many respondents, but others took the view that there was no clear way of enforcing such control and that an educational approach should be followed.

SNH considers that the educational route is the correct one. Through this there should be emphasis on the prime responsibility of dog owners to minimise the effects of their pets. That sense of responsibility should extend to not taking dogs to places where, or at times of the year when, their impact is greatest. SNH's guidelines on this matter are as follows:

–Visitors' dogs should always be on a leash when on fenced farmland. Dogs should also be on a leash when taken on open country during the lambing season and the nesting season.

Ideally, dog owners should not take their dogs at all to places such as Nature Reserves or onto farms with livestock, or other places where birds might be disturbed at the critical time of the breeding season.

CYCLING AND HORSE–RIDING

Cycling has regained popularity; indeed in recent years more cycles (2 million plus) have been sold annually in Britain than motor cars, yet many of these cycles are little used because of fears of safety on the roads. Although most of the cycles sold recently are mountain or all–terrain bikes, the greater part of cycling is still done on the public road system.

Cycling is a valued recreation and a fine way to travel through the countryside, but more action needs to be taken by Roads Authorities to assist cyclists, in particular to facilitate safe access from towns on to the rural road network. There is also a need in many places for separated provision for cycling away from busy roads, to provide for greater safety and enjoyment. Sustrans has provided a strong lead in creating longer–distance cycle–ways, often using redundant railway tracks.

SNH will continue to assist appropriate schemes for recreational cycling, subject to inevitable constraints on resources, since good–quality provision for cycling requires high standards of construction linked to roads engineering. A shift in personal transport from the car to the cycle – especially for the large number of short journeys – would help to reduce demand for more expenditure on roads and have environmental benefits. This can only happen if action is taken to make cycling more attractive. This kind of provision should be met mainly from the roads budgets, because of the close link between cycling and the road network.

Off–road cycling has also grown in popularity and has raised some concerns, in part because it is sometimes practised in ways which do not show sufficient courtesy to other people. These are problems which should be addressed by education and management – indeed, with the Scottish Sports Council, SNH has already supported a code of good practice for off–road cycling.

Off-road cycling is not a new phenomenon. Some people have long taken bikes along hill tracks and drove roads – an activity sometimes called rough–stuff cycling – and this has been done to the extent that a *de facto* 'right to cycle' may exist on some of the long–distance tracks through some glens. Practised with consideration, off-road cycling is an activity which can be welcomed; but where numbers are high or where the more athletic forms of mountain biking prevail, cyclists should be separated from other visitors engaged in quiet enjoyment.

Of all the groups seeking use of paths and tracks, horse-riders are the least well provided for. Safety is a crucial factor for horse-riders. Once the main means of non–pedestrian travel, horses have been driven off the public roads with little provision made for them elsewhere and with few rights of way asserted for equestrian use.

Horse-riders need better facilities.

ATTITUDES TO ACCESS – KEY RESEARCH FINDINGS

The public are less confident in obtaining access to the countryside than is often assumed. In general, people tend to feel uncertain about where they can go and anxious lest they cause problems. Some key findings in a survey of attitudes to access follow.

–People feel confident to go on three kinds of land: 93 per cent of respondents said they would always feel free to go onto the seashore, and 71 per cent to go to lochshore or riverbank, and 63 per cent to moorland and mountains. Very few said that they would feel free to go onto fields with animals or crops.

–Many people have concerns about being out in the countryside. The most prevalent concerns mentioned by those who go walking were of being attacked or molested – about half the sample; of having an accident – around two–fifths of the sample; about getting lost – about a third of the sample; and about knowing where they are free to go – about a quarter. Female respondents expressed much higher levels of concern about most of these issues than males.

–Most people – around 70 per cent – said that they tended to go back to the same place for their walks. The main factors which influenced them in doing this were force of habit, the convenience of using known routes and safety.

–In being asked to respond to some statements about attitudes to access, most people (70 per cent) thought that the countryside should be opened up more for the public to walk in and a majority thought they had a right to go where they liked on moorland and mountains. In general, people did not feel that they were very welcome on land: about half the sample said that they found it difficult to know where they could go; and 70 per cent of respondents agreed with a statement that farmers and land owners are put to a lot of trouble by people coming onto their land.

Although some people will travel with their horse to ride in safe places, most riding is local to private or commercial stabling and the need is for appropriate circuits or access onto land where riding can be accommodated. Stables can place heavy demands on local tracks, sometimes causing conflicts with walkers, and this issue should be carefully addressed through planning and management. Increasingly, there is a move towards riders paying for access but more provision could be made by authorities, especially in protecting equestrian rights of way.

The Roads (Scotland) Act 1984 makes it an offence to cycle or ride on a pedestrian right of way. Not all pedestrian rights of way are suitable for other uses, but this legislation interacts awkwardly with the common law on rights of way and needs re–examination (see Annex II).

Shared use of paths between walkers, cyclists and riders can also cause problems. This is a complex matter which can raise concerns and disputes, and it is one which needs to be examined carefully according to the route, the numbers of different users, and the capacity of the track surface to bear multiple use. Whatever the outcome pedestrians, as the most vulnerable, should always have precedence and the cyclist should give way to horse riders. More information is needed to guide management on shared use.

In summary on riding and cycling, SNH concludes that:

–**More separated provision is needed for cycling and horse-riding and SNH encourages local authorities to take action.**

–**SNH will continue to assist good proposals to enhance opportunities for recreational cycling and riding, but for cycling it looks to the Roads Authorities to play the main role, as most cycling is done on the public roads.**

–**Separated provision will sometimes be needed; but where this is not feasible, care will be needed by all users, the general principle being that the walker, being the most vulnerable user, has precedence.**

–**SNH will promote advice on considerate use of paths and tracks by cyclists and riders.**

PROVIDING FOR ALL

In Chapter 1 SNH identified the importance of positive action to assist people who are less able, disadvantaged or disabled to have good opportunities to enjoy the outdoors. The range of needs here is extensive, ranging from social and physical limitations to perceptual fears about personal safety when out in some places in the countryside.

It is essential that all buildings and related facilities such as car parks be fully accessible to the infirm and disabled, and that a positive approach should be taken at all the formal, managed recreation sites to make part of them accessible to all. The wider countryside cannot be modified to make it generally accessible, but it should be an aim that no one with disability should be limited by artificial barriers (for example, an awkward stile) from reaching or extending their own physical limits. Providing for all requires a positive but common sense approach allied to thoughtful design and management of facilities.

–**SNH will aim in 'Paths for All' to promote the need for integrated provision for people with special needs to assist them to have good opportunities to enjoy the outdoors.**

LINKS WITH LONGER ROUTES

There are in Scotland three official Long Distance Routes (LDRs) established under Section 39 of the Countryside (Scotland) Act 1967: the West Highland Way, the Southern Upland Way and the Speyside Way; in addition, the Pennine Way has its last few miles on this side of the Border. A Great Glen Way is at present under preparation. There are several other promoted long distance walking routes, such as the Clyde Walkway or the Fife Coastal Path, but there are also many traditional long distance routes, especially those following old drove roads or rights of way through the hills. Some of these are very popular, like the Lairig Ghru.

The evidence of how far people like to walk, and our knowledge of the use of the official Long Distance Routes, make it clear that long walks are favoured only by a minority of walkers, some of whom want to travel by using the traditional walking routes to make their own way through upland Scotland or along the coast. Long Distance routes are an important part of the range of walking opportunities in the countryside: they provide assured, managed access which is valuable for visitors to Scotland; they allow people to undertake a challenging venture which they might not otherwise have done; they can be important to local tourist economies and they can act as flagship provisions in local access strategies. The LDRs are also used for many short walks, in part because they sometimes follow routes where such use predated the LDR, and in part because assured, waymarked and promoted access attracts people.

SNH is at present reviewing long distance routes in Scotland. Their purpose should be to provide opportunities for an extensive journey and a high quality experience appropriate to their national status. Many of the new ideas for long walking routes may not meet the criteria needed for national status but they may have the potential to serve local or regional needs and could become important for tourism. Care is needed in the assessment of such proposals, because the market for longer challenging journeys is limited, and the creation and management of such routes can be costly.

Long distance routes should provide a high quality experience appropriate to their national status.

Barriers caused by neglect or lack of welcome all contribute to a people not feeling confident about being in the countryside.

Scotland's uplands inspire and command great affection...but they support land uses on which sparse rural communities depend...and some upland environments can be damaged by over-use for recreation.

Much of Scotland can be classed as upland country, including the valuable areas of hill ground close to the main conurbations.

CHAPTER 3

FREEDOM OF THE OPEN HILL

This chapter presents SNH's views on access to moor, hill and mountain country and considers some of the main recreation management needs there.

Most of Scotland – as much as three–fifths of the land area – can be classed as open country. This land has great recreational value for its openness and wildness and, in the Highlands, for its mountainous qualities. Even central Scotland is as much upland as lowland, and many of these hills – such as the Pentlands, the Ochils and the Lomonds – are of special value for recreation because they lie close to the main conurbations.

There are many other small areas of open land in the Scottish countryside used for recreation. The concern of this chapter, however, is with the sweep of moor, hill and mountain which in all its different moods – rugged, bleak, dramatic and expansive – inspires and commands great affection. But this terrain also supports land uses which are economically fragile and on which many sparse rural communities depend. Some upland environments can be damaged by over–use for recreation. So an approach based on the guiding principles for sustainable use is important.

THE TRADITION OF ACCESS TO OPEN COUNTRY

There is a strong belief among Scottish people that by tradition they have open access to hill country. Legally, however, the general position on access is that no one has a right to be on another's land without consent; equally, no wrong is done when a person is on land peaceably and is causing no damage. Widespread customary use of open land, and acquiescence to this

NTS mountain properties offer a long-standing welcome.

by owners, add up to an implied liberty for people to use hill and mountain land for peaceful open–air recreation.

The ease with which this traditional liberty is exercised varies from place to place. Certain public and voluntary sector owners, such as the Forestry Commission and the National Trust for Scotland on its mountain properties, offer a long–standing welcome and invitation to entry, and so do some private owners. Other individual and institutional owners merely tolerate visitors. There is some legal opinion to suggest that where there is an invitation or open tolerance, the effect is to create a *de facto* permission which means that users are not trespassers and are thus free to enjoy their visit, just as if they were there by more formal right. The legal position on this is not clear.

To some people the Scottish 'tradition of access' simply equates with their own enjoyment of the liberty. For others it expresses an expectation that people should be free to enjoy the commons of life – fresh air, wildlife, fine scenery – as a moral right, because they are 'owned' by no one but are in the joint stewardship of land owners and society. Others consider that generally unrestrained access to hill land only reasserts some earlier freedom enjoyed by local people, at least up to the nineteenth century.

Although the matter continues to be sensitive, comments on access to open country in the responses to the Consultation Paper proved to be less polarised than might have been expected. People who use the hills for recreation recognised that they have responsibilities to others. Land owners and managers generally accepted the requirement to accommodate an acknowledged social requirement, although they expressed concern about the increasing use of hill land and were opposed to any change to the law.

Despite this apparent convergence of view, many walking and climbing organisations raised concerns about the arrangements for access to open country. These organisations and individuals commented that their customary access to hill land now appears to be at risk from increasing restrictions, or from incoming owners who are not acquainted with or sensitive to the traditions. Some of the key recreation bodies came to the view that it is now time to consider creating a legal freedom of access.

One particular issue – which applies to all land, not just the open hill – was uncertainty and disquiet over the landowner's authority to use such minimum force as is needed to make people leave land when they decline to go on request. The law on this is unclear, as the relevant case law dates from the last century and does not relate to recreation.

GENERAL APPROACHES TO ACCESS TO THE OPEN HILL

The sense of tradition underlies a widely held belief that Scots should feel free to walk on their native heath. SNH believes, however, that the way forward on access to the open hill should not rest primarily on appeal to the past. Practical and relevant solutions are required which fit today's needs.

Our approach rests upon the following three principles:

–A sharing of the hill: Through visitors going to the hill for open–air recreation, practice has evolved over a long period which has led to a shared use, and the acceptance of their presence by many (but not all) land owners and managers. An approach of tolerance and sharing is important and it should be fostered so that people can feel free to be on open land. It is equally important that this liberty be exercised with courtesy, showing care for the interests and operational needs of those who live in the countryside and earn their living there.

–Land management needs must be protected: Management for hill farming and sporting uses in hill country is difficult, often undertaken against a hostile climate and in rough terrain. These traditional uses of the land are an important part of the fabric of rural life, helping to sustain communities which are often small, remote and economically fragile. Such enterprises cannot easily bear the extra costs imposed by unwanted disturbance or damage. Most of the upland land uses are extensive and the timing of many essential management operations is limited to short periods, leaving much of the year open for shared use; but restraint by visitors is needed at the critical times of the year.

–The quality of the natural heritage must be sustained: Over–use of hill country can have adverse environmental impacts – for instance, where trampling damages fragile high montane heaths or vegetation on wet, peaty soils. Disturbance to some montane birds is a problem in the nesting season, especially from dogs off–leash.

Overall, the impact of recreation on the natural heritage is not serious, although sustained use of high ground results in some attrition of its qualities of naturalness. These signs of increasing damage – for which there are no easy remedies – underline the need to apply the guiding principles of sustainable use; in particular they call for approaches which minimise impact and encourage visitors to avoid the places most sensitive to damage.

The key to future success in reconciling open–air recreation with other interests lies in the promotion of:

–Thoughtfulness and care from people going to the hill, both to respect the operational needs of land owners and managers and to protect the natural heritage.

–Greater tolerance by land owners and managers of reasonable expectations for access.

–The adoption of appropriate management practices which will increase the capacity of the land to absorb visitors.

These should be furthered by encouraging more responsibility and courtesy, and by making people better informed about upland land uses, about the environments they enjoy so much and their potential impact on them.

The adoption of appropriate management practices is essential.

FINDING THE BEST SOLUTION

Existing statutory agreements: The Countryside (Scotland) Act 1967 gives powers to local authorities (and since 1992 to SNH) to enter into Access Agreements to open country for open–air recreation, and there is also provision for Access Orders where agreement cannot be reached. These powers were adopted directly from existing (1949) legislation for England and Wales and had their origin in an earlier debate (mainly south of the Border) about the need to improve access to open country.

It was envisaged that these powers would provide a basis for agreeing access over extensive areas of moorland and mountain, but they have only had limited use for this purpose throughout Britain. SNH has records of just over 50 Access Agreements in Scotland, some of which have now lapsed. None of these agreements has been made to secure access over extensive areas of hill land; most are for small areas, mainly to allow a local authority to engage in management, or to enable a ranger service to operate. No Access Order has been promoted.

There are several reasons why these powers have been little used: these include the complexity of the legislation, a reluctance on both sides to engage in the formality and commitment required by this kind of agreement, and the limited compensation available to the land owner. In general, the problems of access on open country have not been so severe that agreements have been needed. Also, some local authorities may have been unwilling to enter into agreements for access over open country which would include limitations on the public's use of it and which, by thus undermining existing concepts of freedom of access, would not be acceptable to their elected members.

A change in the law? As described above and in Annex I, people on land without consent will generally be trespassing, although committing no wrong if they are behaving peaceably. The use of land for recreation thus has no clear basis in law and this fact – allied to the sense of tradition described earlier – persuades some people that there should be a legally defined right of access to land. While some think that there should be a right of access to all land, subject to restraints for privacy or management needs, the majority of those who take this view seek a right only over the open hill.

SNH has considered carefully the implications of and the options for such a major change in the law. A change would certainly create greater assurance in access for the public, but there are difficulties in defining and applying a right of access. If there were to be many statutory limitations on when, where, what for and how recreation could be exercised as a right, the outcome could in some respects be more restrictive than the present approach grounded in custom. The main point here is that a statutory solution would have to address matters which are at present left to discretion.

After careful consideration of the implications (see Annex III), SNH sets aside at present the option of a general change in the law to create a right of access; rather, it favours building on existing tolerance and co-operative working. The recently agreed

The Letterewe Accord provides a welcome example of practical co-operation between an owner and recreation interests.

Letterewe Accord [see page 47] provides a welcome example of practical co-operation between an owner and the walking and climbing interests. Chapter 1 set out broad principles which SNH believes should underlie future approaches to access; for three reasons these are particularly pertinent to a voluntary approach to improving access to hill land:

First, the route of improving access through formal agreements has been little used. Second, there is little evidence of widespread restrictions on people using the higher hills. Therefore a major legal change should not be considered until it has been shown that a vigorous effort to promote a voluntary approach has not worked in the places where difficulties persist. Third, a statutory solution could leave land owners and managers with little protection for their legitimate operational needs unless complex (and probably unworkable) restraints were to be built into the law.

However, most people on land are in the position of being trespassers and potentially subject to the use of 'reasonable force' for their removal. More people than ever are now resorting to the hills for recreation, and they are often there as a consequence of the promotion of other public policies, for instance for tourism, sport or education. Society places high value on the importance of open–air recreation, but confusion reigns when the law strictly considers visitors to be trespassing when on hill land. It is SNH's view that people should be free to walk on open country and feel confident that, when acting with care, they are doing no wrong. To this end, SNH thinks that it is now time to re–examine the scope for removing the stigma of people being trespassers when visiting open country for peaceful open–air recreation.

The matter has been highlighted by debate about Section 62 of the new Criminal Justice & Public Order Bill (1994), which introduces a new offence of aggravated trespass. While the declared intention of this legislation is to address specific criminal activities not connected with recreation, it has been perceived by many recreational groups and individuals as significantly shifting the balance of opinion and tolerance which underpin the present use of open land for recreation. There is also a concern that the new law could be used as a basis for more aggressive warnings or notices to visitors, thereby making the countryside less accessible by being less welcoming. SNH understands these concerns.

The Secretary of State has provided an assurance that this legislation will not affect the position of mountaineers, hill-walkers and ramblers, all of whom do not come within the intended scope of the provision provided that there is no intention by them to disrupt lawful uses of the land. SNH welcomes the positive statements and action by the Scottish Landowners' Federation to try to ensure that owners do not see this law as an opportunity to curb access taken reasonably.

These assurances, however, may not be sufficient to allay fears among recreational visitors and to sustain the necessary climate of goodwill between them and those who own and manage the land. Accordingly, SNH believes that a legislative change designed to clarify the status of the innocent visitor would help to bring the legal position more closely in line with the reality of present day use of open country for recreation, and to lay the foundations for improved access based on co-operation. This change should clarify that people on open country (as defined in the Countryside (Scotland) Act 1967) are not regarded in law as trespassers unless required to leave by a proprietor (see Annex II).

As the law stands at present, owners have a right in certain circumstances to ask people to leave their land. The use of force, or threatening or aggressive actions which cause people to be alarmed, is widely regarded as an inappropriate way of securing the removal of people who are on land peaceably for open–air recreation. SNH believes that the law which permits private individuals to use reasonable force – or such minimum force as is required – to remedy a civil wrong by securing that people on land leave is now outmoded and, on account of the nature and paucity of case law precedent, uncertain. This matter should be reviewed. Visitors should not be fearful of meeting an aggressive confrontation if they are acting in a responsible manner (see also Annex I, paras 5-8).

SNH concludes that:

–**A general change in the law to create a right of access to open hill land should not be pursued unless and until it can be shown that a vigorous effort to follow a voluntary approach is not securing improved access in places where there are currently real problems.**

–**Debate on the Criminal Justice and Public Order Bill has brought into sharp focus the status of the 'innocent trespasser'. This makes it all the more desirable to identify legislative changes which, if introduced, would remove the stigma of most visitors being trespassers when in open country.**

–**The use of force or other aggressive actions should have no place in the exercise of an owner's right to ask people engaged in peaceful open–air recreation to leave their land, and the law on this should be clarified. SNH intends to hold discussions on the above recommendations with the key interests.**

–**Overall, the best way forward for the present is to build on existing approaches to co-operative working between recreation interests and land owners and managers.**

There are several examples already of good co–operative action and of goodwill towards working for better access through consensus. The access guide *Heading for the Scottish Hills* (1993) is the outcome of joint working between the Mountaineering Council for Scotland and the Scottish Landowners' Federation. The Letterewe Accord has been welcomed as an example of good local action; and the SLF has promoted an Access Pact as a central proposal in its own access policy statement, *Towards Access Without Acrimony* (1993).

Building on these welcome actions, SNH proposes:

–A national Concordat on access to the open hill, to set out mutual responsibilities and basic principles to guide free and responsible use of open hill land for recreation.

–The establishment of an Access Forum to provide a continuing means of liaison on the general issues and principles of access, and to debate and seek resolution of the key access issues of the day.

These proposals are outlined below.

THE CONCORDAT APPROACH

A national Concordat would have the main purposes of helping to promote the voluntary approach and to establish the basis on which both visitors and land owners and managers would feel comfortable about access onto hill land. This is now urgent, given the changing patterns and increased numbers of people going to the hills. The Concordat would be signed in the first instance by the main recreation organisations, the landowner organisations and the main public bodies involved in promoting access. Commitment to the principles of the Concordat might be displayed individually by landowners, who would in this way promote a welcoming approach to access.

The Concordat would be a set of broad principles, the main elements of which would be:

–To affirm that individuals acting responsibly are welcome to use open land freely for quiet open–air recreation;

–To express a commitment to meeting reasonable public aspirations to access and to promote a 'walkers welcome` approach;

–To reassure land owners and managers that their operational land management needs and their personal need for reasonable privacy (and that of others who live and work in the hills) will be respected.

–To confirm that existing rights of way and traditions are to be respected.

AN ACCESS FORUM

An Access Forum will seek to build bridges between recreational and land owner and manager interests, especially to help with better understanding of each others' needs, and to debate how best to accommodate them. It is intended that the Forum should address access issues for low ground and other settings; but initially it will focus on the open hill, because there are evident opportunities here to develop co-operative working, and the necessary goodwill already exists to promote early action.

Preliminary soundings with the main representative bodies for recreation and land owning, and the relevant public bodies, have indicated support for this proposal and the Forum has now been established with an initial membership appropriate for open hill matters. The membership of the Forum will be small in order to promote effective working; balanced, so that there are roughly equal numbers of the recreation groups, the land owning interests and the relevant public bodies; and representative, mainly of the 'umbrella' organisations which can inform and consult their own constituencies about the Forum's work.

For open country the Forum's first main task is to draw up a detailed Concordat. The broad purposes of the Forum for the open hill are therefore:

–To agree the wording of a national Concordat on the principles of access to the open hill and to give a lead to its adoption.

–To promote good practical working between recreation and land management interests, in particular to develop a code of practice for recreational use of the hills to back up the Concordat.

–To debate and resolve at a national level any general problems of principle which arise from recreation on the open hill.

–To affirm a joint intention between parties to enhance the quality of upland environments and to protect the interests of communities.

–To make a commitment to address any difficulties through discussion and compromise.

THE MAIN RECREATION MANAGEMENT NEEDS IN THE HILLS

Use of the hills for recreation has grown over recent decades, assisted by a greatly improved roads network and increased promotion through guidebooks and the media. This has led to great enjoyment for the hill–going public; but in the most popular hill areas, for example on the Mamores or on the Ben Nevis hills, public recreation can now be the main *de facto* activity on the land – although this is not the owners' purpose for holding the land and no benefit is gained by them.

The use of the hills for recreation has grown over recent decades.

The management of access and of recreational impact in upland country needs a sensitive touch, in order to respect the natural qualities of these places, to recognise that it is a working environment, and also to respect the perceptions of the users who seek freedom and relaxation in natural settings. Some approaches to management will have to find remedies to the physical impacts of access. Other approaches are educational, and some will involve more planning of a strategic or tactical nature, for instance to promote the long walk in or, where feasible, to encourage more use of places of higher capacity to withstand the impact of recreational activities.

An agenda of what needs doing should be created through discussions at the Forum and through more general consultation and debate, but some of the main issues are as follows.

A footpath repair team in action.

–Repair of upland paths: In the most popular areas the hills now show signs of wear and tear from public use, manifested in damage to access paths and in the development of continuous worn ground along ridges. This kind of impact is also beginning to be seen on the less visited tops. Generally there is not enough repair of paths, except on the mountain properties of the National Trust for Scotland (which has taken a commendable lead in this work). Elsewhere the private owner cannot be expected to carry the burden of maintaining paths which are primarily used for public enjoyment.

SNH has already made a commitment to more effort to care for upland footpaths and has sponsored surveys of what is needed in Skye and Wester Ross. Also, substantial grants have been given by SNH – and by its predecessor CCS – for path works throughout upland Scotland including some major reconstruction schemes, as on Ben Lomond. Welcome supplement to this grant has been provided by the Scottish Mountaineering Trust from the proceeds of its guidebook sales. Well designed and maintained paths are important in helping to contain damage. But there remains much to do, essentially meeting the invoice for past decades of growing recreational use of the hills and little previous investment to remedy its effects.

SNH will work with its other funding partners, particularly the local authorities and the LECs, to identify and assess the repair needs of upland paths, to fund specific projects and to promote good advice on methods of path repair.

–Deer stalking and hill-walking: Continued effort is needed to promote accord between hill-walkers and climbers and the other land uses. A main need here is to create better communication and understanding between hill–walking and deer–stalking interests. Over large areas of the Highlands deer–stalking is a main economic use of the land, and there is increasing concern among land owners and managers that more people on the hills are either affecting the distribution of deer or making it more difficult to stalk without risk of disturbance.

There is a need for better understanding between hill-walking and deer-stalking interests.

The evidence on disturbance to stalking is limited, but the concern is about the continued increase in numbers of walkers and the growing risk of disturbing an activity for which the clients of the sporting estates pay highly. These revenues from deer-stalking are a major contribution to local employment and the rural economy. There is also a general consensus that the numbers of red deer on the open hill are too high and should be reduced for a number of good reasons, including the need to reduce over–grazing to protect and enhance the natural heritage.

A general ban on access to the hills over the shooting season (which begins in the middle of the main tourist season) would not be acceptable or even workable. Aggressive notices warning visitors off are also unwelcome. The main approach should be educational, to promote better understanding of the needs of deer management. Walkers and climbers going to the hills over the main period of the shooting season will also need to show consideration by avoiding the main stalking areas at critical times. Equally, more information for walkers is needed of when and where stalking is being done and suggesting alternative destinations.

The Access Forum will take a lead in promoting accord between deer-stalking and hill–walking interests through action to promote understanding of the issues and to reduce conflict by other approaches.

Scotland's uplands have a high value for nature conservation.

Avoiding impact on wildlife: Scotland's uplands have high value for nature conservation. Some places are recognised as having international importance and are increasingly being protected by designation, such as Special Protection Areas under the European Union Directive for Birds and, in the future, the EU Directive for Habitats and Species. There may be a growing need for caution in the recreational use of some of these areas but, on present evidence, the impact of recreation on these valuable places and the consequent need for any restraint are limited.

Solutions to any problems of this kind are most likely to be found by promoting among walkers and climbers a better understanding of the impacts of their activities and in working closely with recreational interest groups to reach mutually acceptable solutions. The individual has a role to play in avoiding key locations at the sensitive times (as in agreements for climbers to avoid cliffs with breeding birds) and in keeping dogs on the leash when on hill ground in the nesting season.

Where problems arise from access in managing nature conservation in the uplands, SNH will seek mutually acceptable solutions with recreational interests. Where recreation is having an adverse effect on any site, some restriction on recreation may be required.

Improving accessibility: The accessibility of open land outwith the main areas of the uplands – for instance, to the smaller blocks of hill country in central Scotland – is often limited by physical constraints, such as the lack of parking space or obvious routes, or by the need to cross enclosed land or pass through a farm steading, or by intimidatory signs.

Local authorities, in particular, need to do more, in discussion with land owners and managers, to secure better access through enclosed land to assist people to reach open country, and to achieve this without causing new problems.

As well as better management to remedy the impact of visitors on the hills, there is a parallel need to continue to protect and enhance the qualities which make Scotland's uplands so attractive for open–air recreation. People who seek their recreation in the hills place a high value on their wildness. Remote and wild places often provide sanctuary for important wildlife, as well as being valued by their owners for precisely the same qualities which give enjoyment to visitors. But 'wildness' is sensitive to external change, such as by increased accessibility and promotion of the hills, by development in remote places or new private roads for land management, and by more people visiting such places.

THE LETTEREWE ACCORD

Some of the finest mountain scenery in Europe is found on the Letterewe Estate in Wester Ross. It is renowned amongst hill-walkers and climbers for its wild land qualities. The Letterewe Accord is a set of principles which aim to enhance public awareness of wild land needs and to provide a guide to its use and enjoyment, both on Letterewe and perhaps elsewhere in the Scottish Highlands. The Accord has been drawn up by Letterewe Estate in co–operation with outdoor organisation representatives. It has developed from discussions initiated by the Mountaineering Council of Scotland and the Ramblers' Association with the Estate.

Fundamental to this Accord is the recognition that all who visit, or live and work on the land and water of Letterewe, must cherish and safeguard the area's wildlife and beauty. Such places are increasingly rare in a world where the natural environment is under ever growing pressure. A new approach is needed. Co-operation between individual and community interests in the sound management of wild land is one element. It reaffirms that human needs are inseparable from those of the natural world.

–The prime objective at Letterewe is to maintain, expand and enhance the area's biological diversity and natural qualities. This will ensure that these are central to the experience of all who visit the area and are recognised as an essential element in sustaining the long-term economy of Wester Ross.

–Red deer management policy is based on selective culling, aided by scientific research, with the aim of maintaining population levels appropriate to the regeneration of the natural habitat.

–All who visit the area are asked to recognise that red deer stalking is carried out across most of the estate area with the most important period being weekdays from 15 September to 15 November. Visitors are asked to contact the estate during this period for further advice.

–Visitors are encouraged to base their visit to Letterewe on the concept of 'the long walk in'. Adequate experience, training and equipment to meet the rigours of travel in this remote area are essential.

–Public use is based on the tradition of freedom of access to all land, subject to any agreed modifications for conservation or management reasons.

–There are footpaths through those areas where there are benefits for land management or for visitor access.

–Car parking, telephone and other facilities are available at Dundonnell, Kinlochewe and Poolewe.

–The estate does not favour the construction of new vehicle tracks or the use of all terrain vehicles. Ponies and boats are used for estate management.

–Mountain bikes should be used only on existing roads or vehicle tracks and not on footpaths or surrounding land.

–Minimum impact techniques should be used when camping overnight using lightweight tents. Pollution and disturbance to wildlife, especially sensitive lochshore birdlife, must be avoided.

–Visitors are encouraged to visit the area in small, rather than large groups.

–Research studies which help to further understanding of the use and protection of wild land are welcome at Letterewe.

LETTEREWE ESTATE WILL BE PLEASED TO ADVISE ON ANY ASPECT OF ESTATE MANAGEMENT AND ON WAYS TO MAKE ANY VISIT TO LETTEREWE AS ENJOYABLE AND REWARDING AS POSSIBLE

THE LETTEREWE ACCORD
produced by Letterewe Estate in association with

John Muir Trust
Mountaineering Council of Scotland
Ramblers' Association Scotland
Scottish Wild Land Group

December 1993

Better management for open–air recreation, and better care of places valued for recreation, call for a more integrated approach to management across the different uses of the uplands.

WILD CAMPING

One access issue which deserves specific attention is wild camping. Camping wild in open country has long been enjoyed by walkers, climbers, canoeists, cyclists and others involved in open–air recreation. Putting up for the night in an independent manner is a traditional and valued part of the recreation experience. When done with care, by small numbers of people, no problem arises.

As car–borne tourism grew in the 1960s, the practice of roadside camping increased and, over the years, this has continued to create problems of pollution, litter and loss to amenity. There are also concentrations of camping away from the road in particular places favoured by climbers or walkers, and the same kinds of problems arise around heavily visited bothies. While camping away from the road appears to have grown in recent years, there is probably less roadside camping now than there was in the 1970s: there are now more formal campsites, there has been better management of some of the previous concentrations of wild camping.

Under the 1865 Trespass (Scotland) Act, camping (and also the lighting of fires) is an offence without the owner's consent. It has long been the view of open–air recreation organisations that this is both a heavy–handed and an inappropriate law, as the original purpose of this statute had nothing to do with recreation. Yet this law is still in use in cases of encampment which create public nuisance, and has come into prominence recently in use against New Age travellers.

Wild camping done responsibly has been tolerated by many owners and SNH proposes that under the Concordat this practice of tolerance should continue and that genuine recreational camping following an agreed code of practice should not be a matter for prosecution. There are, however, continued anxieties among owners, and also some recreation interests, that concentrations of camping do cause local problems. It is timely, then, to promote a code of practice for wild camping, and the Access Forum will consult with recreational bodies and others on the framing of such a code. A basis for this code is set out on page 50.

As car-borne tourism grew in the 1960's the practice of roadside camping increased, leading to problems of pollution, litter, and loss of amenity.

–**Under the Concordat, SNH proposes that lightweight mobile camping practised with care and following a code of practice should not be a matter for prosecution but be recognised as an integral part of the enjoyment of the outdoors.**

–**A code of practice for wild camping should be developed and promoted through the Forum, in concert with all the relevant parties.**

TARGETS

The Forum has now been set up. Our targets for the implementation of the other main action points in this Chapter are as follows:

–**The terms of the Concordat should be agreed by the main parties by early 1995.**

–**A revised code for the use of open hill land should also be prepared within twelve months of the publication of this report.**

–**By the year 2000 there should be general coverage of open hill land by 'walkers welcome' arrangements analogous to the Letterewe Accord.**

–**Proposals for clarifying the legal position on people being in a state of trespass and on removal by force should be ready for discussion in two years.**

–**SNH should lead a review of the success of the Concordat approach by the end of the decade.**

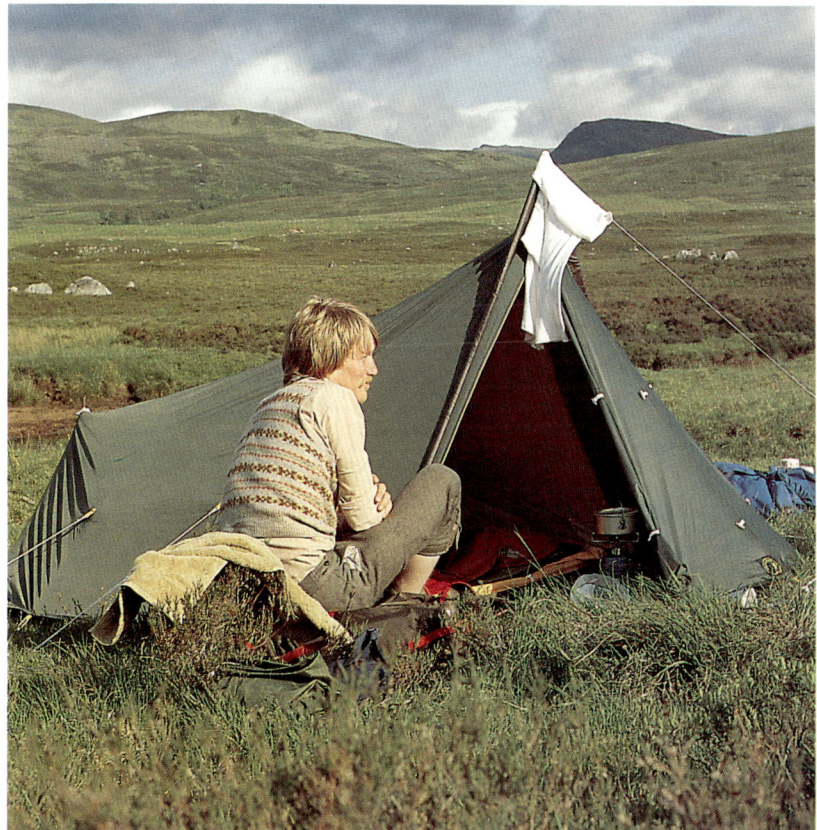

Done with care, wild camping in open country causes little impact.

AN OUTLINE CODE OF PRACTICE FOR WILD CAMPING IN OPEN COUNTRY

Camping wild in open country is one of the great pleasures of open–air recreation. Done with care it has little impact on the countryside. But as more people use open country for recreation, more thought and effort are needed to minimise the impacts which camping can cause, to maintain the quality of the experience and of the popularly–used sites. By putting in extra effort to disperse away from popular or convenient places, by following best practice and by showing consideration to others' interests and concerns, we can continue to enjoy camping with minimum impact.

–**Always camp more than 500 metres from a public road and avoid camping less than 1 kilometre from any private dwelling without seeking permission.**

–**Stop in one place for no longer than 2 nights.**

–**Camp in small groups only and, to spread the impact, avoid regular use of the same place.**

–**Choose a site which is dry, safe and unobtrusive, but do not modify it by moving boulders, digging drainage ditches or removing vegetation.**

–**Show restraint in not camping in places where your presence might disturb wildlife, or in scenic spots where tents would be intrusive.**

–**Camp at lower altitudes where your impacts on vegetation will recover more quickly; but if using high ground, avoid sensitive vegetation such as moss heaths.**

–**Avoid having fires and, however you are cooking, avoid any risk of setting fire to adjacent vegetation or woodland. Be especially careful in dry, Spring weather, when there is often much dead and tinder–dry grass to fuel moorland fires.**

–**Take away every single piece of litter. Never leave (or bury) any food scraps, as these attract scavenging animals and birds.**

–**Be careful in your personal hygiene. Do not foul sites within 50 metres of any water course; dig a shallow hole and bury human waste – but do not do this under boulders.**

Forests provide a sense of seclusion and shelter, can absorb large numbers of people, and can provide opportunities for sports such as mountain biking, orienteering and car rallying.

Forestry policy recognises that recreation is an important part of multi-purpose woodland management.

CHAPTER 4

FORESTRY & WOODLAND

This chapter reviews the important role played by access to woodlands and forests in providing space for a wide range of recreations.

Scotland's forests and woodlands play a particularly important part in the provision of public access. They have a robustness, both physically and ecologically, which contrasts with the fragility of many other vegetation types; their networks of paths and roads are accessible and safe for walking, cycling or riding. They are important for recreations which depend on a woodland setting, such as orienteering, and for others which would be less easily accommodated on open ground.

Above all, forests provide a sense of seclusion and shelter and can absorb large numbers of people. The fact that major management operations occur at infrequent intervals means that public access does not need to be regularly interrupted. It is widely accepted that access by the public for informal family recreation, especially for quiet walking, creates little difficulty and involves slight expense. While fears of increased major fire risk from public access have declined, constant vigilance against this serious danger will always be important.

The capacity of woodlands, especially the larger forests, to absorb bustling activities such as competitive mountain biking,

and highly intrusive events such as car rallies, is important because there are few other locations where these pursuits can be easily accepted. The accommodation of intrusive recreations in woodlands is not a matter for SNH unless they would lead to damage to valuable habitats, as has happened in some places from War Games, or where they intrude on valued settings for informal recreation. These will normally be commercial activities and SNH recognises that there is a demand for them.

Forests are a valued component of our landscape and offer important opportunities for access and recreation.

THE FORESTRY COMMISSION

The Forestry Commission has played an important leadership role in woodland recreation, providing an excellent welcome to the general public for peaceful informal recreation and accommodating many active pursuits as well as catering for the enjoyment of wildlife [see below]. As early as the 1930s the first National Forest Park was being created and a greatly expanded network of facilities now provides highly valued opportunities for public enjoyment, such as small picnic areas and woodland walks as well as general open access. The Forestry Commission (and now Forest Enterprise) have made a major contribution to the provision of facilities for informal recreation in Scotland, particularly in tourist areas.

RECREATION FACILITIES – FOREST ENTERPRISE

Scotland now has six Forest Parks – a non–statutory designation applied to extensive areas of forest and associated land managed for multiple benefits with particular emphasis on recreation; they are Glenmore and Queen Elizabeth Forest, Argyll, Galloway, Tay and Borders, spanning over from England. In addition there are nine Woodland Parks – another Forest Enterprise designation which is applied to smaller parcels of land managed by Forest Enterprise where public recreation is a prime management objective; they comprise Craig Phadrig (Inverness), Dàlbeattie (south of Dumfries), Dunnottar (Stonehaven), Glentress (Peebles), Kilmory (Lochgilphead), Kinnoul Hill (Perth), Mabie (Dumfries), Quarry Wood (Elgin) and Scolty (Banchory). Forest Enterprise has also designated five forests as Caledonian Forest Reserves: the Black Wood of Rannoch (Tayside), Dalavich Oakwood (Loch Awe), Glen Affric, Glenmore (Cairngorms) and Glen Nant. The first three of these are among the 17 Forest Nature Reserves; in these, interpretive and educational facilities are encouraged, with an emphasis on visitors with a special interest in wildlife.

National forest policy envisages all Forest Enterprise properties as multi–purpose forests, and the government encourages the development of native woodlands as part of this strategy. The Forestry Commission's *Forestry Policy for Great Britain* (1991) stated:

'Forests and woodlands are an integral part of the rural environment, providing important opportunities for recreation and for public access to the countryside. They are also a valued component of our landscapes and an essential habitat for wildlife ... Multi–purpose use is an important aspect of present forestry policy. The emphasis has widened from encouraging timber production to the provision of social and environmental benefits arising from planting and managing attractive, as well as productive, woodlands.'

The Forestry Commission's policy of open access and its evident welcome to visitors allows people to know they are free to walk in these forests and consequently to feel relaxed and confident.

DISPOSAL OF FOREST ENTERPRISE LAND

The provision of improved access for countryside recreation requires that the opportunity provided by forest areas should be increased, regardless of ownership. Many of the respondents to our Consultation Paper expressed concerns about the loss of access opportunities both from possible change in the status of Forest Enterprise and the continuing programme of disposals. Government created a mechanism which theoretically would achieve continued public access to woodlands sold to the private sector in the disposals programme. It is regrettable that the record of maintaining public access to Forestry Commission (now Forest Enterprise) land after disposal has been so poor: between 1981 and 1993 some 51,000 hectares of state forest in Scotland have been sold but, with only a few exceptions, there has been a failure to safeguard public access to it. This is a matter of concern.

SNH regards it as vital that public access to woodlands which have been disposed of should be fully assured in the future. SNH is calling for an increase in the provision of public access to privately owned land in the uplands and in the enclosed farmland of the lowlands; the same principle should apply to forests established with the help of substantial public investment, many of which are now entering the maturing phase in which the value for public recreation is becoming all the greater.

Following a wide–ranging review, the Government has confirmed that Forestry Commission woodlands will be kept in the public sector and under a single management structure. This is beneficial for access because it is the totality of Forest Enterprise's provision – the amount of access, and its location as well as its quality – which creates such high value for the public. Helpful too is the increased funding the Government has promised to support the arrangements for securing continued access to woodlands sold to the private sector.

However, it remains to be seen whether these arrangements for securing future access will be sufficient. The objective should be that public access is assured on conditions closely similar to those in public forests in the rest of Europe: open and welcoming access, with provisions for its temporary withdrawal for timber working, woodland regeneration, fire risk and conservation reasons.

- **It should be a guiding principle of the Forestry Commission's disposals programme that the degree of access enjoyed by the public under the present customary arrangements is safeguarded and only subject to restriction on operational grounds or for the protection of natural heritage interests.**

PRIVATE SECTOR WOODLANDS

The public has long enjoyed the privilege of access to woodlands and forest roads on the traditional private estates, especially the larger ones. The Forestry Commission's figures on recreational visits by the public to woodlands indicate that, in Scotland, nearly as many visits are made to woodlands in the private sector as to those in state ownership.

In the large new forestry plantations created by the forest management companies recreational access is also important, although the type of welcome offered by the Forestry Commission has not been so

Private sector woodlands play an increasing role in welcoming the public.

conspicuous, and the public may often be uncertain as to whether they may enter plantations which are not in state ownership. There are signs, however, that this is changing as these forests mature, and as forestry interests respond to public need.

–SNH welcomes initiatives by the Timber Growers Association and the Royal Scottish Forestry Society to encourage the private sector to expand recreational opportunities and will offer support and guidance to such proposals.

In view of the difference in scale between the larger forests and most farm woods, it would be both inappropriate and of little value to the public to try to apply the same general principles to every piece of farm woodland which has received Woodland Planting Grant, since there is often no convenient access to the edge of many of these small woods. Indeed many farmers would be reluctant to create woods on their farms if there were a likelihood that public access would be required, since that would often complicate farm management; this would represent a significant potential loss to the natural heritage. But where recreation opportunity in small woods is welcomed by owners, this should be encouraged.

In the Forestry Commission's surveys of visits to woods, local authority owned woodland emerged as playing an important role, probably because many of these woods lie close to settlements or in parkland. Access to woodland is particularly important to local communities, and new grant support for Community Woodlands [see below] offers the prospect of improved access arrangements in the private sector. In addition to the creation of new environments for leisure and learning, Community Woodlands offer a chance to add interest and diversity to the landscape of the surrounding countryside, the creation of new habitats for wildlife and the opportunity for active local involvement in the management of the woods. SNH welcomes these new woods, and Government's support of them, as places for people to enjoy and to identify with as 'their own piece of countryside'.

COMMUNITY WOODLANDS

The Forestry Commission launched its Community Woodlands initiative in 1992 with the aim of encouraging the planting, close to our towns, of a range of new and diverse woodlands which can be used for informal recreation. Planting approval as a Community Woodland attracts a grant at higher than normal rate from the Forestry Authority, to offset the higher costs of design and establishment. Proposed Community Woodlands must be within five miles of the edge of a village, town or city and be within an area where the current opportunities for woodland recreation are limited. They should be of reasonable size and are more likely to be accepted if they form part of a series of such woods, perhaps along a footpath, or form part of a larger recreation development such as a Country Park.

Grant for creating Community Woodlands is paid as a supplement as part of the Woodland Grant Scheme (WGS).

Woodlands provide peaceful settings for people to relax in, and to enjoy many pastimes.

Community Woodland Supplement is paid as a lump sum with the first instalment of WGS establishment grant for new planting. The Supplement is only paid if free public access (on foot) is allowed, although there usually needs to be appropriate car parking close at hand.

In 1992/93, the first year of the initiative, 19 schemes covering 232 hectares were approved by the Forestry Authority. In 1993/94, 30 schemes were approved, covering 285 hectares. Uptake is better south of the border; there, during the two years of the initiative, 2,300 hectares have been approved.

–**SNH welcomes the Community Woodlands initiative and will work with Forest Enterprise to help local communities to promote them within the context of the 'Paths for All' initiative.**

THE CENTRAL SCOTLAND WOODLANDS INITIATIVE

One of the principles of SNH's approach to access is to facilitate provision nearer to home. While the Central Belt now provides growing numbers of access opportunities (Regional Parks, Country Parks and other facilities) there are no major access arteries or networks, and to many settlements the surrounding countryside presents a cold shoulder.

A major opportunity exists in Central Scotland as part of the Central Scotland Woodlands initiative [See below]. Purchasing land, restructuring its ownership and planning and implementing environmental improvement through tree planting is only one approach. Local communities could well be in a position to take over the management of some of these areas in the future. Another possibility is the development of Community Woodlands (see above), where the provision of access (on foot) is an essential condition of grant.

THE CENTRAL SCOTLAND WOODLANDS INITIATIVE

The Central Scotland Woodlands initiative aims to achieve an environmental transformation between Edinburgh and Glasgow through the development of the new Central Scotland Forest which will comprise a mosaic of farmland, settlements, open space and woodlands with the traditional elements of harvestable timber, mixed species planting, open and closed canopy and recreational provision. An essential element of this initiative is therefore to create and ensure the continuation of public access to new and maturing woodlands. This can be accomplished in a number of ways, some of which are already being taken forward by the Central Scotland Countryside Trust, a body core–funded by SNH on behalf of the Government, in partnership with the Forestry Commission, the local authorities, Scottish Enterprise National and the local enterprise companies.

A number of abandoned railway lines and stretches of canal present an opportunity to develop a major access spine in the area and could stimulate a series of local networks. The completion of open–cast coal extraction projects will also create access possibilities, as do the water–supply reservoirs which are no longer required; these offer opportunities for access to water (see Chapter 5) and for the creation of woodland on the surrounding land.

–SNH, as the Government's agent and major funder of the Central Scotland Woodlands initiative, will seek to ensure that access opportunities associated with the creation of the new Central Scotland Forest are achieved.

EUROPEAN MODELS

Forest practice in continental Europe offers useful lessons in access provision and management. Over virtually all Europe, forests are open to the public, both those publicly and privately owned; as they cover a substantial proportion of the land areas of most of the countries concerned, this is an opportunity of considerable significance. In general this public access is a right or is regarded and treated as such and it is exercised with care and self–discipline. It is normal in most countries in Europe for the land owner to be able to withdraw temporarily the right or privilege of access from parts of the forest for the purposes of planting or regenerating, for nature conservation reasons, or for timber harvesting.

A well sited carpark screened by trees.

A quiet path through the forest or wooded landscape is often all that is required.

Scotland has superb water resources... a magnificent and diverse coastline and many inland water bodies which are rich in wildlife and under increasing recreational and commercial uses.

Water is the venue for many recreations, from quiet enjoyment at the water's edge to active pusuits on the water.

CHAPTER 5

THE COAST AND INLAND WATER

The coast and inland waters of Scotland are hugely attractive for recreation. This chapter considers access to and over water.

Water is the venue for many recreations, from quiet enjoyment at the water's edge to active pursuits on the water, some of which are challenging and venturesome, or involve competition. Scotland has superb water resources – a magnificent and diverse coastline of the highest importance to wildlife, and western coastal waters of great value for sailing. There are large and mainly unpolluted river systems and a considerable number of inland water bodies of all sizes and in very varied settings. The demand from recreation to have access to this water resource is increasing, as is exemplified by the problems at Loch Lomond and the Trossachs lochs which were reviewed recently by the Government's Working Party for this area.

Water–based recreation has a number of differences compared to the equivalent use of land. First, the extent of the inland water resource is much more limited and, while Scotland is well endowed overall with water space, its distribution is uneven so that some areas are short of local water for recreation. Inland water is normally under use for multiple purposes, including economic uses such as water extraction, sport and game fishing, or other commercial forms of recreation; accommodation has to be found between these and conservation needs as well as providing for public enjoyment.

Pursuits which use water are generally active and dependent on specialist equipment and they sometimes require exclusive use of part of the water surface. There is demand for water space from motorised water sports, and these can create the most difficulties, mainly in disturbance to other quieter pursuits. Management on the water surface can be difficult to implement. On the most intensively used water bodies there is often good practice in zoning and sharing use, but this requires goodwill, a commitment to adhere to codes or local rules and also an element of supervision. Often good management of this kind comes in

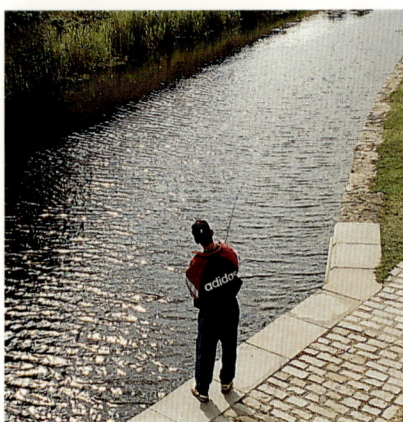

Access to the waters edge is greatly attractive to the visitor.

after problems have arisen, either between different recreations or between recreation and economic uses.

The law of access over inland water does not match today's needs; the range of legislation which governs fishing and poaching, and the different systems of managing water, all add to the complexity. Some of the recreation interests on water lie beyond SNH's remit as many of the activities pursued on water fall under the aegis of the Scottish Sports Council, so SNH can only offer interim views on access over water as further debate is needed.

However, the broad aim of securing improved access over land should also apply to water and the water's edge. But there is a need for care in the integration of recreation with the economic uses and conservation needs. Inland water which is unused or only lightly used for recreation is an important part of the tranquillity of the countryside, as well as providing sanctuary for easily disturbed wildlife.

–There should be improved opportunities for access over water – inland and coastal – and to the water's edge, but special care is needed to integrate these arrangements with the other uses of water, especially for inland water.

ACCESS TO THE WATER'S EDGE

The water's edge – marine or inland – attracts greatly for its natural qualities; it is a zone rich in wildlife which is often of special interest, and there is the attraction of expansive outward views. The water's edge is a dynamic zone, prone to change from the natural forces of wind, wave and changing water levels, and damage can sometimes arise from over–use for recreation.

Access to the coast or the margins of inland waters is a form of access over land, except that there is a common law public right of access for recreation on the foreshore – between tidal limits – but a legitimate means of access to the foreshore is needed to enable this right to be enjoyed.

The attractiveness of the water's edge for informal recreation is demonstrated by data on the location on walks gathered in the survey of walking for the Review (see Annex IV). Almost a quarter of walks (23 per cent) were along a beach or cliff–top and a further 11 per cent at the edge of inland waters – river, loch or canal. About one–third of day trips made by Scottish residents to non–urban locations are to the coast. Accessibility is a crucial factor in enabling the public to get to the water's edge as access to inland waters is often over fenced land. Improvements to access here should draw from the principles set out earlier for path networks.

The coast is often open land, normally with no other major economic use. There is longstanding and traditional public use of the accessible parts of the coast, which is reflected in the common law right to use the foreshore for recreation. In the north and west, and on the islands, the coast is often the bounding edge of the uplands and access is not a major problem, except for the remoteness and roughness of such terrain. Elsewhere, access

Access to water is a crucial issue for the active pursuits.

may be over farmland or croftland where routes to the sea are sometimes neither obvious nor promoted.

The status of most of the coast as open country puts it alongside the open hill as part of the countryside where people should feel free to go. The main reasons for possible local and seasonal restraint to cliff and rocky shores are for conservation (bird roosts), and occasionally for safety. But soft coastlines of dune or saltmarsh are significantly less able to withstand heavy recreational use. Estuarine flats and saltmarsh do not attract large numbers of people but, because of their dynamic and fragile nature, sandy coastlines require careful resource management where recreational use is heavy.

As far as is reasonable, a general freedom of access along the coast should be secured; indeed in some areas – for example the Fife Coastal Path – provision for this is being planned. Formal access of this kind is important, but the wild and unmanaged character of the remoter Scottish coast should be preserved.

–**Access to the edge of inland waters is important in arranging access through fenced farmland, but subject to the needs of land management and wildlife. Planning and management for access to the water edge is an issue which should also be addressed in strategic planning for open–air recreation.**

–**Access to the open coastline for quiet enjoyment should be generally available, subject to any limited restraint needed for conservation management and public safety.**

THE LAW OF NAVIGATION

At sea (and over estuaries to the High Water Spring Tide point) there is a general right of navigation. A right of navigation has been asserted through the courts for the Rivers Spey and Leven only, but continuing use of many rivers and water bodies for recreation may have created such a right on a more extensive basis. Litigation to assert this would be contentious, potentially expensive and in no one's interest.(Annex I)

It would be premature, however, to recommend change to this complex state of affairs. Whatever the imperfections of the legal position, it is the case – as on land – that effective progress is best made, not by recourse to the law, but by discussion and compromise, and by recognition of the legitimate interests of others. The need for a planned and managed approach to satisfying needs for water recreation points to general approaches such as promoted in Chapter 3 for open country through a Concordat. It is for this reason – as well as the special complexity of the law relating to water – that SNH does not at this stage make any detailed recommendations on possible changes to the law.

The matter should be debated further in the light of a vigorous effort – as for open country (Chapter 3) – to secure acceptable solutions through co–operative working. The Access Forum will have an important role to play in this.

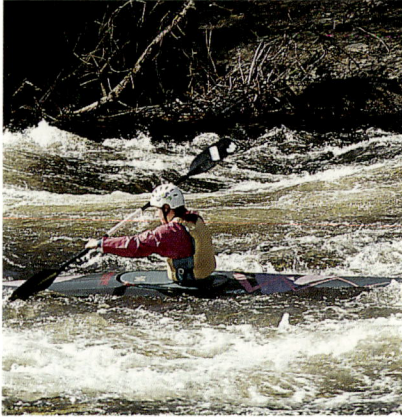

–The law on access over water for recreation by the public does not accord with today's needs, but further debate and further effort to promote co–operative working on access are needed before determining whether changes are appropriate.

PLANNING AND MANAGEMENT FOR WATER–BASED RECREATION

The management of access to inland waters raises five main issues: improving accessibility; the operational problems of undertaking management; interactions with riparian and other water–use interests; the ecological value of these places; and the interactions between different recreations.

Resolution of these issues as they arise locally will need negotiated solutions involving all the parties. It is likely that co–operative working over water recreation may best be done by river catchment, although in some areas, where the level of recreation is heavy, special solutions or mechanisms involving a public body in the lead will be needed (as for Loch Lomond and the Trossachs lochs).

–SNH encourages a co-operative, planned and negotiated approach to access for water recreation which should be integrated with other elements of water management.

Except for water bodies owned by them – usually as reservoirs – most local authorities have not become greatly involved in the general management of water recreation. Where they have intervened, one difficulty lay in establishing byelaws for inland water bodies under the Civic Government Act; but this problem has now been resolved through an amendment in the current Local Government (Scotland) Bill.

The different recreations using water all have their own needs, which should be accommodated through negotiation.

Elsewhere, mediation over access and management (especially for angling) is often a matter of direct negotiation between the recreation interests and the owners. This can be a constructive way forward but it carries the risk that groups negotiating access can secure their own exclusivity.

Where unmanaged public recreation over water becomes obtrusive, a degree of anarchy can seem to prevail in a few places. Sometimes there can be safety risks to people, perhaps from unwise mixing of different recreation activities exacerbated by inconsiderate behaviour (usually by only a minority of participants). The Loch Lomond and Trossachs Working Party debated these issues and recommended that, for this kind of setting, strong planning and management–based solutions are needed to resolve problems both on the water and at its edge.

The special factors associated with water recreation – the diversity and local intensity of uses, the need to accommodate multiple use, and the scarcity in some areas of water space – all point to the need for a more strategic approach. Broadly–based discussion is required with all the interests, sometimes involving adjacent authorities, to promote strategic zoning for more intensive use of water for recreation.

–SNH believes that the local authorities should play a stronger role in the planning of access to and over water and in contributing to its management wherever significant problems of use are emerging.

For motorised water sports a broader national strategy is required, because noisy water sports can spoil the essential tranquillity of the countryside. Their practice can be incompatible with other recreations and inappropriate in locations of high natural heritage value. Concerns were expressed in the responses to our Consultation Paper that pressure on water space south of the Border may now be causing an influx to Scotland of motorised activities, decanted from lakes and reservoirs in the South, where controls are now in place. Reasonable opportunity needs to be created for recreations of this kind, but without compromising others' interest in quiet recreations or disturbing natural heritage interests.

While this issue is not yet a major problem in Scotland it would be wise to address it now, given that activities of this kind are promoted by advances in technology making new forms of water craft more widely available.

Motor-based water sports need more zoning and management, and a planned approach.

–SNH recommends that provision for motorised water sports be guided by a national strategy and it will promote discussion on this.

In the responses to the Consultation Paper, SNH received representations that the recreational needs of the public should be safeguarded in the forthcoming changes to the organisation of the public water supply. SNH agrees that this is important. Access for recreation at public reservoirs, and also to related open land, is important. In some cases it involves Country or Regional Parks. Many of these reservoirs are located in or close to the Central Belt, where the greatest demand for recreation exists and where there is sometimes shortage of opportunity for water recreation. Existing reservoirs have a crucial role to play in meeting demand close to where most people live. SNH has already made this point in its own initial submissions to government on the proposed changes. SNH's policy stance is as follows:

–Changes to the arrangements for the administration of public water supplies should not lead to reduction of opportunity for recreation (water and land–based) by the public or to existing provision becoming less accessible.

Angling interests have made representations to SNH on access for fishing, particularly on Protection Orders, which continue to raise controversy. SNH is committed to promoting the effective management of natural resources. The Freshwater and Salmon Fisheries Act (Scotland)1976, under which Protection Orders are made, aims to secure better management while maintaining good opportunities for the angling interests. Suggestions were made that insufficient provision is made for review of Protection

Orders. It is for The Scottish Office Department of Agriculture and Fisheries to ensure that this legislation's aim of fair access is being met, and SNH recommends that this be kept under close review.

–Protection Orders under the Freshwater and Salmon Fisheries Act (Scotland) 1976 provide a basis of managing the fishing resource and of agreeing access for angling by the public. It is important that these arrangements allow for increased public access to fisheries, and that they are regularly monitored to ensure that the interests of the angling public are secured.

Lastly, all water recreations can have impacts on wildlife. But many of the representative bodies for water recreation have already prepared minimum impact codes to promote care and restraint in how their activities are undertaken; more action of this kind is encouraged.

A dolphin awareness campaign shows good practice in promoting care for wildlife.

Water provides the backdrop for many recreations for all ages.

Providing for countryside recreation has been under funded in the past... a greater commitment is needed from public bodies involved in promoting or managing open-air recreation, and funding from new sources such as the National Lottery could be harnessed.

More planning and management is needed, both to improve the quality of provision for enjoyment of the outdoors and to protect the qualities and values which make Scotland's countryside so attractive to open-air recreation.

CHAPTER 6

ROLES AND RESOURCES

This chapter considers the roles and responsibilities of the different organisations and interest groups which play a central role in funding, promoting and managing open–air recreation.

Providing access to the countryside for open–air recreation is costly and has been underfunded in the past. A bolder effort is required, which brings together greater commitment by the range of public bodies involved in promoting or managing open–air recreation, and which harnesses funding from new sources, such as the agricultural support schemes (Chapter 2), and from the bodies which promote tourism and from the National Lottery.

In responses to the Consultation Paper, most people were of the view that the costs of providing for open–air recreation should be met from sources funded by general taxation. The idea that the general recreational visitor should pay directly for access is generally perceived to be not only impracticable but also inappropriate. It is a long–established part of our tradition in Scotland that there should be no charge for the enjoyment of fresh air, nature, and fine landscapes. Most open–air recreation involves short local walks dispersed through the countryside. Participants do not pass through any kind of turnstile where revenue could be collected, although charges may be made for services, such as car parks, or through entry to special facilities.

–Enjoyment of the countryside for open–air recreation should be without charge, although charges will be appropriate where specific services are provided.

The roles and responsibilities of some of the main players in improving and promoting access are considered below.

Providing for all in a country park.

Ranger and fisherman, Strathclyde Country Park.

A Highland Region ranger helps a visitor to enjoy the outdoors.

THE ROLE OF THE LOCAL AUTHORITIES

Local authorities involvement in leisure and recreation has expanded greatly in recent decades. A review by SNH of expenditure by the authorities on open–air recreation indicated that it still commands no more than 5 per cent of leisure and recreation budgets, and that the levels of such expenditure are significantly lower than are being applied by local authorities elsewhere in Britain to this work. A high proportion of that expenditure is on the managed facilities – the Country Parks, Long Distance Routes and Regional Parks. The local authorities also have to meet many of the costs of recreation and tourism in the rural areas by providing basic services and infrastructure through their roads, environmental health and other budgets.

Much of the local authority expenditure on open–air recreation has been supported by grant from SNH and the former CCS under the Countryside (Scotland) Act 1967. Grant has been an important catalyst in helping to provide basic infrastructure for local access, such as car parks, toilets, roadside picnic sites and so on. A ranger service – now 160 strong and also supported by SNH grant – provides an essential field force to manage and mediate locally on access, to advise and provide interpretation for visitors and to care for their safety.

SNH recognises that local authorities have the central role in the planning and promotion of open–air recreation. Although facing reorganisation in the short term, only the local authorities have the long-term continuity, the relevant statutory powers, the workforces, the democratic remit and the local knowledge and connections to take the lead.

The forthcoming reorganisation provides an important opportunity for the new authorities to give a stronger focus to how they deliver their functions for open–air recreation. SNH believes that this is an activity which can best be promoted through the new authorities having strong countryside management teams or units which operate across departmental interests to integrate recreation provision, planning, conservation management and links with rural tourism.

The authorities' ambitions for open–air recreation should be expressed through strategies for countryside recreation. This is primarily a land–use planning activity which can be presented as a non–statutory plan, although some authorities may prefer to make a formal link with the statutory plan system. Effective plans of this kind should also have linked programmes of action. Progressively, SNH will want to allocate grant for recreation by reference to planned programmes, rather than by responding to individual applications. SNH believes that such plans should provide the basis for enhanced contributions from the authorities' now significant leisure budgets.

–SNH affirms the central role of local authorities in planning and providing open–air recreation in the countryside, and it calls on them to invest more in this work. The key roles of the authorities are as follows:

taking a lead in strategic planning for open–air recreation in their areas – the new authorities should prepare strategies for open–air recreation for their areas which should link with or may form part of their statutory plans;

expanding their present efforts in managing the formal facilities for open–air recreation to the highest standards – the Country and Regional Parks, as well as car parks and small picnic sites;

leading increased action to promote better local access and to protect rights of way (given simplification of the present system); and

generating action through collaboration with a range of funding partners, including SNH, and by working closely with land owners and managers.

THE ROLE OF THE TOURISM ORGANISATIONS

Open–air recreation in Scotland has an important place in tourist development and promotion. The Scottish Tourist Board and the Development Agencies have contributed greatly over the years to the provision of many built facilities and improved accommodation for tourism. Their main local successors – the LECs – have followed on in this work; but there has been much less investment in the care of the natural resources used by tourists for their enjoyment.

Tourism is now a highly complex and fiercely competitive international market. Scotland's valued outdoor resources, serve important markets such as the enjoyment of fine mountain and coastal scenery, opportunities for active pursuits, a rich diversity of wildlife, and a distinct social and cultural history, as well as field sports. All these outdoor activities depend on the quality of natural heritage.

The marketing of Scotland for these pursuits has become much more sophisticated and targeted, and also increasingly successful. But there has also been general disquiet about some of the drawbacks of tourism and travel such as damage to fragile ecosystems (especially as evidenced abroad) and this has led to the development of 'green tourism' ideas and policies. In Scotland these have found expression through the Tourism and the Environment Initiative, led by the Scottish Tourist Board, in which SNH is closely involved and which it warmly welcomes.

The arrangements for public sector support to tourism development have now been devolved to the local level, mainly through the LECs as part of their core responsibility for local economic development. Some interesting local initiatives to improve access have emerged through the LECs and have involved SNH locally, such as appointment of a Borders Walking DevelopmentOfficer. SNH welcomes the interest of LECs in stimulating local action for access. It is important that this is undertaken in close collaboration with the local authorities, especially to ensure that new capital projects do not leave the authorities with unreasonable, long–term maintenance commitments.

Scotland's outdoors -its scenic and cultural values are of great importance to tourism.

Ferry to Iona

Port Askaig, Islay.

Path management is costly, but needs more effort.

This is a crucial issue because much of the funding for access takes the form of revenue costs, or as a capital requirement to upgrade the quality of places long without maintenance following years of heavy use by visitors. Ways should be explored to enable those bodies which promote tourism to contribute to the ongoing revenue costs of managing for improved access. This is especially important in Highland Scotland where the local authorities have to meet the costs of providing services for the visitors attracted through national tourism promotion.

Bodies promoting tourism should also contribute to the care of the natural resources affected by their activities through adopting stronger policies and practices based on the principles of sustainability. These should aim at influencing the tourism agenda so that it does not lead to increased burdens on other land uses or to escalating impacts on the natural heritage or on rural communities.

SNH's broad approach to the involvement of tourism in open-air recreation is as follows.

–**SNH gladly acknowledges the high value placed on the natural heritage, and the recreation opportunities in it, by people who come to holiday in Scotland; it also recognises the importance of tourism to the rural economy of Scotland.**

–**Tourism organisations have a responsibility to contribute to the care of the qualities of the natural environment through planning for and marketing tourism in ways which follow the guidelines of sustainability – especially in recognising that those parts of our natural environment which are least able to tolerate heavy use should not be promoted.**

–**In welcoming the Tourism and the Environment Initiative, SNH stresses that increased funding will be needed to contribute to the care of places heavily visited by tourists.**

–**SNH welcomes the involvement of LECs in investment to improve access for tourism and local use, and encourages more of this. Investment of capital in this way should recognise the revenue implications and the need to upgrade the quality of existing provision in the busy tourist areas.**

–**Through the provision of information and interpretive services for visitors (and training to this end), tourism can play an important role in helping visitors to understand better the importance of our natural heritage and can also help to promote an ethic of care in its use.**

THE ROLE OF THE VOLUNTARY SECTOR

A great variety of voluntary bodies is involved in recreation. They range from major national organisations like the National Trust for Scotland, which owns and manages to a high standard some of the most outstanding areas of Scotland's countryside, to bodies which represent and lobby for outdoor sports and recreations. There are also many special interest bodies, like the Scottish Rights of Way Society, the John Muir Trust or Sustrans, which have access for open–air recreation close to the centre of their purposes. In addition there are many clubs and other organisations which represent participants in recreation at the local level.

These bodies face increasing pressures, sometimes to act in a public service role because they are specialist in their field, or because they all have the difficulty of representing their own interests in a more complex world. This can demand high standards of professionalism and heavy commitment from the individuals who act as voluntary office bearers. The role which all these organisations play in open–air recreation has been crucial, not just in promoting recreation itself, but also in action to conserve the resources which they use for their enjoyment.

Voluntary bodies can play an important role in promoting good practice by their members and through voluntary effort in assisting local maintenance – a way of putting something back into care for the resources they use. Some of the representative bodies have become closely involved in detailed negotiation and debate about local access issues on behalf of their members, and they can be well placed to do this.

SNH welcomes this trend and affirms its support for the distinctive role which all these organisations play – whether in managing land, representing their recreational interests or in contributing to the care of the resources they use.

–SNH welcomes the important role which voluntary bodies play in recreation. SNH will continue to assist these organisations – as it has done in the past – especially to undertake well–conceived projects which help reconcile recreation and the other interests in land or water used for public enjoyment.

–Clubs and other voluntary organisations involved in open–air recreation should consider new initiatives to put 'something back in' through voluntary action to help manage or care for the resources they use.

–Representative bodies are encouraged to prepare and promote codes of good practice to encourage a minimum impact approach to the practice of their activity, and SNH will assist them to do this.

OWNERS OF PUBLIC LAND

Many government agencies and other public bodies (including SNH) play important roles in open–air recreation, because they hold or manage land or water used by the public and to which visitors are welcome.

The Forestry Commission stands first, because of the extent of its landholdings in Scotland and the amount of good quality provision already made for informal recreation, especially in the tourist areas. This role – and SNH's concern about threats to it from the disposals programme – is discussed in Chapter 4. Many other public bodies and also some private utility companies previously in the public sector have been prepared to welcome the public onto their land or water. SNH does not expect to assist public sector bodies through grant (because they are also funded from the Exchequer), but it wishes to endorse and commend their role in providing better access for the public and to encourage greater commitment to this.

–SNH commends the important contributions made by many public bodies owing and managing land in providing for public access and it calls on them to continue this commitment as an important public service role as a demonstration of good stewardship and integrated use of their properties.

–Privatised utilities should adopt a similarly welcoming approach. The transfer to the private sector of public bodies owning land or water should not result in opportunities for recreation by the public being diminished or made less accessible.

PRIVATE LANDOWNERS

The role of the land owning community in enabling open–air recreation is crucial. SNH greatly welcomes the positive stance adopted by the Scottish Landowners Federation in promoting broad–based policies which recognise the needs of society for access for open air recreation. Other bodies representing land owning or land use management interests also made positive statements in their responses to the Consultation Paper. SNH values this commitment and encourages them all to promote such messages widely to their members.

Fitting open–air recreation in and around private land management needs is sometimes not easy, especially on more intensively used land. But with goodwill, and with appropriate management and support where problems arise, SNH believes that it should be possible to meet public needs alongside the private and economic uses of land. This should be the way forward.

–SNH encourages the representative bodies for land owning and land management interests to continue to promote to their members recognition of the public's need for access for open–air recreation.

THE SCOTTISH SPORTS COUNCIL

Scotland's outdoors is of huge value to participants in the active pursuits, many of which fall under the aegis of the Scottish Sports Council. There have been trends towards increased participation in the active pursuits, to the diversification of some of these activities, and to higher standards of performance and practice. There is much more training in these activities and strong policies are promoted to this end.

Active outdoor recreation has a long history: climbing and cycling go back well into the last century and skiing dates back to the turn of the present century. The main early mountaineering clubs and cycling organisations have now

Provision for water sports needs a planned approach.

passed their centenary. Horse–riding for enjoyment is much older still. Today the range of active pursuits using the natural heritage has expanded greatly and participation has increased many times over. Many of these activities are pursued informally and there are many participants who are not affiliated to clubs or other sports organisations. Some of the activities often involve competition under the supervision of the governing bodies for sport, which set high standards for the conduct of events.

Not all outdoor sports enjoy ease of access, especially where the activity conflicts with other land uses or with other recreational interests or values. In these cases – such as noisy motor sports – a more strategic and planned and zoned approach is needed, both locally and at the national level. The Scottish Sports Council is the appropriate organisation to take a lead in this work.

A greater contribution is called for from the bodies which promote active sports in the countryside to help in the management of the resources used for these activities and in the mitigation of any problems which arise. High standards of provision and management are very properly applied to formal sports facilities in towns and cities and a considerable level of resources is applied to this. Parts of the countryside are now subject to fairly intensive use by active sports and more funding should be directed to its management and to promoting a minimum impact approach to the practice of these activities.

–**Broad policies for active pursuits lie within the remit of the Scottish Sports Council. SNH welcomes the fact that the Council will be preparing a strategy for countryside sports in the forthcoming revision of its main policy statement *Sport 2000.***

–**Access for active pursuits which may conflict with other land uses or with other recreations should be addressed through a planned approach, led nationally by the Scottish Sports Council.**

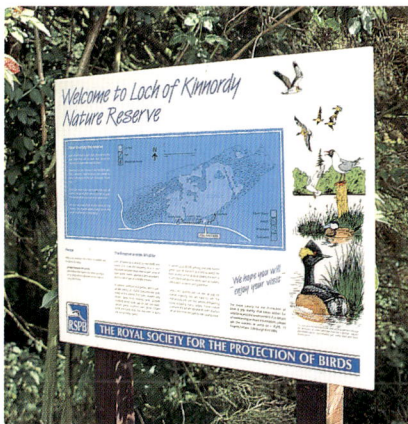

OUTDOOR EDUCATION ORGANISATIONS

Voluntary bodies play an important role in welcoming the public.

Enjoyment of the outdoors has long been associated with the study of natural history and this has become a highly popular pastime, as demonstrated by the large membership of the main voluntary bodies for nature such as the RSPB. As interest in the natural environment grows and as higher education expands, there is more use of the countryside for study and training in the natural sciences. Schools, colleges and universities should show care not to put disproportionately heavy burdens on places of special conservation value or on individual land owners or managers. Access to the countryside for education and training is an opportunity for demonstrating and promoting good practice in taking care and showing concern for land management needs.

- **Training and education in the countryside provides an opportunity for demonstrating and promoting an approach of care and respect, especially when training other trainers.**

- **Access for *bona fide* educational purposes should not be a matter of charge, but groups should seek consent and show**

care for land management interests, as well as being mindful
of the pressure which continued use of the places they visit can
put on their value.

–SNH will publish advice and good practice in the use of the
countryside for education and training courses.

Involving young people in the challenges of open–air recreation
has for long been a valued way of helping them in their own self–
development. Increasingly this approach is directed at helping
young people with troubled lives to come to terms with or to
break out from their problems. Policies of this kind are promoted
in initiatives such as the Hunt Report – *Search for Adventure* –
which calls for action to ensure that all young people have an
opportunity to engage in outdoor pursuits. SNH greatly welcomes
this use of the outdoors, but learning to value and respect the
places used for these activities is an important part of the
outcome.

–SNH endorses initiatives to introduce young people to the
outdoors, but it stresses the need for such training and related
experiences to be broad–based, to engender a sense of care for
the natural heritage and to promote understanding of and
respect for the main land uses.

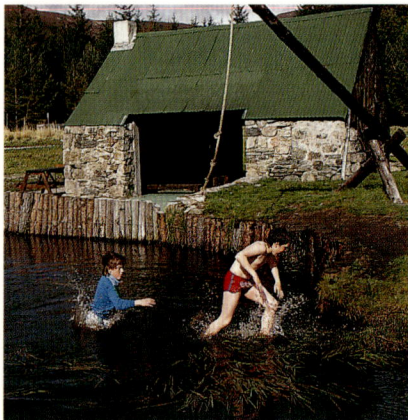

*Badaguish Outdoor Centre,helps young
people with special needs.*

THE ROLE OF GOVERNMENT

The Government's commitment to open–air recreation has long
been reflected in legislation for open–air recreation and through
the provision of funds to facilitate it which are channelled
through its sponsored bodies and agencies or through local
authorities. Nonetheless open–air recreation is sometimes
viewed by Government as a relatively minor issue in the overall
use and management of land. But with the growth of public
enjoyment and the less certain economic viability of some of the
traditional land uses (especially on less productive land),
recreation assumes a greater role in the land use mix. Thus, in
large areas of upland Scotland recreation is now the main land
use, either as a private and commercial use for field sports or in
public use – or the two combined. Yet recreation lacks any clear
status as a land use or assured funding commensurate with its
level of importance to society.

The importance of recreation extends beyond land use. As
already mentioned it is of crucial importance to tourism and the
rural economy. It has importance to the health and well–being of
the nation and in fostering the sense of identity between the
people of Scotland and their country. In the marketing of Scotland
for inward industrial investment, recreation opportunities in fine
environments are often used to illustrate the high quality of life
which Scotland can offer. This link between recreation and the
quality of life is a message to hold on to firmly, because it is an
important part of what makes Scotland such an attractive place to
live.

*Open-air recreation is now a main use of
land in the hills.*

South of the Border, Government has given enthusiastic backing
to ambitious targets to open up the whole rights of way network
by the end of the decade. Scotland has lagged behind in the
provision of this kind of access network. The arrangements in

place for rights of way south of the Border cannot be replicated here, but a major effort is now needed (as set out in Chapter 2) to enhance provision for local access so that a substantial improvement can also be made in Scotland by the year 2000. Government's support for SNH's proposals for 'Paths for All' and for changes to the rights of way legislation is essential to help to secure early progress.

–SNH believes that enjoyment of the outdoors deserves a higher place in national policies, both in recognition of its significance as a major land use and for the economic and social benefits it has to offer.

–In future revision of the agricultural support schemes, the role of open–air recreation should be recognised, both as a benefit to the public accruing from taxpayers, contributions to supporting agriculture and as an opportunity for payments to assist farmers provide for and enhance recreation opportunities.

–Access onto public land (and water) which is sold or privatised should be maintained and enhanced. Opportunities for open–air recreation on other public land should be enhanced wherever possible.

–Improvement of local access requires that the administrative arrangements for rights of way be simplified. SNH urges Government to provide space for such change in its legislative programme.

–Work on rights of way and footpaths should be given support through guidance to local authorities, possibly in a new Circular on the subject.

SNH'S OWN COMMITMENT

SNH's general commitment to improving access is set out under the proposals in earlier chapters. SNH is committed to maintaining its efforts in supporting good work by all its present partners, but others will need to contribute more if the improvements as proposed in the earlier Chapters are to be achieved.

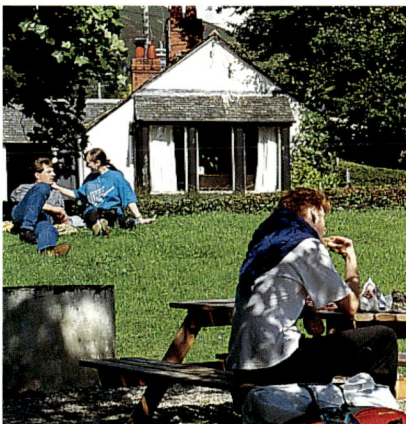

The popular parking and picnic area at Balmaha.

During the 1970s and 1980s financial assistance under the Countryside (Scotland) Act 1967 has been an important factor in providing better facilities for countryside recreation.Some of this assisted voluntary bodies such as the National Trust for Scotland, but many private estates have welcomed recreation, in part to diversify estate enterprise. SNH will continue to assist land owners and managers to open up access and to help them to manage significant access problems on their land.

SNH is also committed to promoting high standards of recreation provision and to encouraging approaches to recreation management which build on the principles of sustainable use of land. SNH will seek to promote good standards through research, by disseminating good advice and by training. SNH will provide a lead in all of this through the management of its own land.

–SNH will maintain its commitment to assist by grant the management of open–air recreation by the local authorities and its other partners, but it will move towards funding programmes of work based on local recreation strategies.

NEXT STEPS FOR SNH

The previous chapters set out an agenda for improving access to the Scottish countryside. Some of the statements are general policy stances, others make recommendations to a range of bodies or state what SNH proposes to do next. SNH will now enter discussions with its main partners and implement a programme of work to develop and promote the details of its new approach. Already, one major proposal – to establish an Access Forum – has taken shape and the Forum has started its work. The initial actions in this programme will be as follows.

'Paths for All' Initiative

Develop the Paths for All initiative by:
–establishing a project team;
–publishing and promoting advice on the development of path networks;
–developing a programme of work to involve local communities in path work; and
–preparing and promoting a targeted incentive scheme for the above. All the above in 1995.

Access Forum

Discuss through the Access Forum and with key partners the form and content of an Access Concordat for open hill land and the way in which it is to be implemented. Agree the terms of a Concordat by early 1995.

Develop general approaches (via the Access Forum) on mediating between hill-walking and stalking and shooting by early 1995.

Develop a package of advice to promote an ethic of care approach to enjoyment of the countryside, including a review of the use of the Country Code in Scotland and the need for supplementary codes and related advice by mid 1996.

Promote access as a component of a broader–based approach to land management support.

Initiate discussions on access over water by early 1995.

Advice, Guidance and Financial Support

Develop and publish advice on grants policy and priorities for recreation by early 1995.

Promote advice on strategic planning for informal recreation. To be published by mid–1995.

Complete internal reviews of long distance routes by early 1995 and rangers by Spring 1995.

Legislative Change

Promote to Government the need for new legislation on footpaths and rights of way.

Partnership Approach

Through the Access Forum, and also in bilateral discussions with key partner bodies, discuss the proposals in this report and how they might be implemented. These discussions are ongoing.

A very wide range of organisations is involved in access. Each has a distinctive and significant role to play. The Access Forum will provide a means of general liaison on broad issues and strategies on access, but SNH will want to continue to meet with other interested parties and to promote action locally.

There is a need to develop a more comprehensive approach to informal open-air recreation at the national level. CCS's policy paper *A Park System for Scotland*, published in 1975, set out a framework for countryside recreation, which was influenced by American thinking about the need for a spectrum of recreation opportunities to serve the full range of public aspirations for enjoyment of the outdoors. Almost twenty years on, this policy is now in need of major revision. This programme for action represents a first and crucial step towards a strategic overview of countryside recreation. SNH will promote a wider framework of this kind in collaboration with other organisations which have parallel responsibilities for tourism, sport and the provision of facilities, as well as with the land owning and managing and recreation interests.

OVERVIEW

This Paper promotes new ways of improving access to the Scottish countryside for open–air recreation. In some ways we have been spoiled in Scotland by the quality of the resources for enjoyment of the outdoors and by there being less crowding of the countryside. Perhaps as a result there has been a perception that somehow there are not so many issues to address.

Comparisons with other countries suggest that this is too complacent a view. We only need to look to mainland Europe and to the generally better arrangements there for access to enclosed land, to woodland and to mountain terrain. These other countries seem to show greater appreciation of the value of such opportunities in contributing to the quality of life and the welfare of society and they make a correspondingly greater commitment to ensuring that these opportunities are widely available. Increasingly, the kinds of standards of provision enjoyed in other parts of the European Union will be seen to be the norm.

We have a large amount of accessible open country, and an outstanding coastline, such that the shortcomings in access opportunities over fenced farmland and close to towns and settlements have been overshadowed. It is close to where most people live, therefore, that the priority must lie. It is too late now to base our provision on a network of definitively mapped rights of way, as enjoyed south of the Border; but with goodwill and increased endeavour much can yet be done through negotiation, to promote an expanded network of accessible local paths.

SNH has set aside for the present the option of major legal change to secure any general right of access to the open hill because we believe that in the present circumstances efforts to secure such a right would be counterproductive. At heart, improving access involves changing attitudes and promoting acceptance of responsibilities by landowners and by visitors alike. This is the route we choose, as being the best way forward to defuse confrontation and to promote effective action. We are clear, however, that the success of this option must be monitored and reviewed by the end of the decade.

This Paper sets out an agenda for better access to the countryside. Let the year 2000 be seen as a target by which time our arrangements for such access should match the best in Europe, in ways which reflect Scotland's distinctive circumstances, needs and traditions.

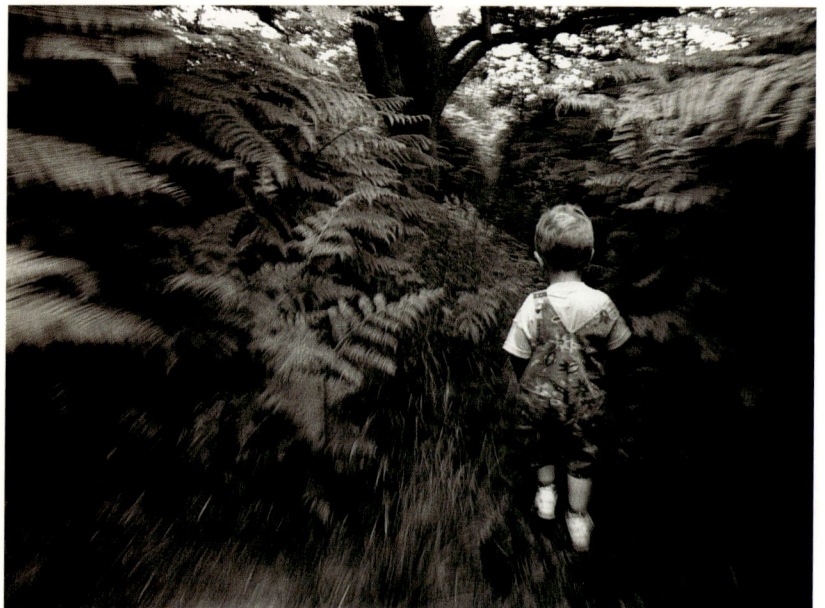

ANNEX I: THE LAW RELATING TO ACCESS FOR OPEN-AIR RECREATION

1.This Annex provides a very brief summary of the main elements of the law relating to access for open–air recreation. It is not an authoritative nor a complete statement and further information and discussion can be found in authoritative legal texts or (for land) in *Public Access to the Countryside: A Guide to the Law, Practice and Procedure in Scotland* (1993), published by SNH. Much of the law on access lies in the common law (that is, law based mainly on principles emerging from authoritative court cases) but there is a shortage of recent case law on access and some aspects of the law are not clear. This is not a summary of the law on recreation, which is much wider than the law on access because it involves many general legal issues.

2.The main statute law on access is to be found in the Countryside (Scotland) Act 1967, which gives powers – mainly to the local authorities – to enter into agreements to provide for access to open country and to create public paths. This Act also gives the local authorities a range of powers to provide for and to manage recreation, such as the provision of Country Parks, or the making of byelaws. Since 1991 SNH may use the access agreement powers.

3.In some circumstances members of the public may be on land by right, for example being in a public place; on a public right of way; on a public path created by agreement; or on land where an access agreement is in force. There is also a public right to be on the foreshore for recreation. There are uncertainties with some of these cases: for example, what the right of recreation on the foreshore includes, or the definition of a 'public place'. Many rights of way have not been fully asserted and may be open to challenge. There is only a small number of footpath creation and access agreements.

4.Most recreational access takes place on land where the visitor has no clear right to be. In these cases, unless the visitor has consent, expressed or implied, he or she is trespassing. Many private landowners, and voluntary and public bodies, do invite the public to enter their land and where there is such an invitation the visitor is no longer a trespasser. There is also a tradition of customary access to land, especially to the open hill, which depends on the acceptance or tolerance by the owner of peaceful recreation by the public, but without any particular welcome. There is some legal opinion to suggest that this may be based on implied or *de facto* consent to the visitor, but the matter is not at all clear.

ACCESS TO LAND

5.Owners may safeguard their right to control who uses their land by requiring a trespasser to leave. The law is not clear on the extent to which owners may use such minimum force as is required to secure the departure of someone who declines to leave on request. The use of force by any side – especially if unreasonable force is used – could itself be a matter of civil or criminal action, depending on the circumstances.

6. Owners may seek an interdict (a court order) to restrain named persons from entering onto their land, but evidence is needed to prove that trespass, or repeat of past trespass, is likely. This provides no way of limiting entry by the transient visitor who cannot be readily identified, or to limit the general recreational use of land. Owners cannot claim damages from a trespasser unless damage to their property can be proven.

7. Trespass can be a criminal offence under statute law where it is associated with some other act (such as carrying a firearm), but most of this legislation does not bear on normal recreational activities. The main exception is the Trespass (Scotland) Act 1865, which creates an offence when a person encamps or lights a fire on land without consent.

8. The Criminal Justice Bill 1994 proposes a new criminal offence of aggravated trespass. The offence arises when a person is a trespasser on land and intentionally obstructs or disrupts a lawful activity or intimidates those involved. This new provision has caused alarm among recreation organisations lest innocent visitors be caught by it. Government has said that persons on land for open–air recreation and acting with care will not be at risk of prosecution, as the new law is aimed at problems of deliberate disruption to activities on land which have no connection to recreational access.

9. The law on rights of way can provide for pedestrian, horse or vehicular use, but use of rights of way for purposes other than walking is not often recorded or asserted. There are very few places where a motor vehicle can be taken off the public road without the consent of owners, as very few vehicular rights of way (apart from the public road network) exist, and it is an offence under the Road Traffic Act 1988 (Section 34) to drive on land without consent, subject to a short–distance limit from a public road, within which vehicles may be parked without creating an offence.

10. The position in law for cyclists and equestrians is that (like other persons engaging in recreation) they will have no right to be on land unless there is a specific right or consent. In addition, Section 129(5) of the Roads (Scotland) Act 1984 makes it an offence to ride, lead or propel a vehicle or horse on a footpath or a footway (a path associated with a road). Under the same Act (Section 151) a footpath is defined as a road where the public right of passage is by foot. There will be many routes where historic use by the cyclist or horse-rider could be claimed against the common law criteria to establish a right of way, but this is seldom done and the gathering of evidence would be difficult.

ACCESS OVER WATER

11. The public have a right of navigation over tidal waters, that is, the sea and estuaries up to the high water spring tide mark. This right includes the right to perform activities which are necessarily ancillary to navigation.

12.On inland (non–tidal) waters, a public right of navigation must be established by demonstrating that there has been repeated public use of the water since time immemorial (taken as 40 years) and that the water is navigable. This follows the notable defence of a right to navigate on the River Spey, which was determined at the House of Lords on appeal and which is now the contemporary reference for navigation. The right of navigation is qualified in that its exercise must be reasonably described as navigation, using a vessel which can reasonably be described as a boat.

13.For rivers, the running water strictly cannot be owned, but the owner's rights extend to making use of the water as it passes by or through his land. Where there is a public right of navigation the owner's rights are subject to that right, but navigation must be exercised in a reasonable manner. Inland lochs are owned by the proprietors of the surrounding land. Generally speaking, they have exclusive rights to the water. The public only have a right to be there if a public right of navigation has been acquired.

14.There are several differences between the law on access over water compared with that to land. For example, access to a water body via one riparian owner's interest can give access to the whole resource; the right of navigation is not lost once established; it is not clear what aspects of recreation on water may amount to navigation; and no public body has a remit to guard rights of passage over water, as is the case for rights of way over land.

15.A right of navigation has been asserted through the courts only for the River Leven (Dunbartonshire) and the River Spey. Elsewhere, sailing etc by the public is by negotiation and agreement, by entry and use, or by a claimed right of navigation where there has been long–standing use.

16.Salmon fisheries are a property right, which may or may not belong to the riparian owner. Fishing for trout (brown trout and also other non–migratory freshwater fish) without the permission of the owner of the right of the fishing is not a criminal offence if done in a way which is legal (and if there is no Protection Order in force), but a person who does this without permission has no right to do so or to be on the land. Some people claim that there is a freedom to fish for non–migratory species, analogous to a freedom to roam. Fishing for non–migratory species can be controlled through Protection Orders granted by the Secretary of State under the Freshwater and Salmon Fisheries Act 1975.

17.Statute law provides some support to the management of access and recreational use of water through the general powers of the Countryside (Scotland) Act 1967, such as access agreements or ranger services or byelaws. This Act also allows (Section 56A) for the control through byelaws of disturbance by engine noise to the enjoyment of quiet areas of the countryside. The Civic Government (Scotland) Act 1982 (Section 121) provides for the regulation of recreational activities through byelaw, both for inland and in near–shore coastal waters. These powers have been little used, although one impediment – the difficulty of obtaining the consent from all riparian owners to byelaws proposed under the Civic Government Act – has been removed through amendment in the current Local Government (Scotland) Bill.

AIR SPORTS

18.Owners have rights in air space above their land although statute law on aviation provides for overflying by aircraft. Apart from the possibility of infringements of an owner's rights, access to air space has two main elements: first, there is the use of land for launching, taking off or landing and this is subject to supervision by the Civil Aviation Authority in licensing sites; second, the use of air space is also governed by the Civil Aviation Authority.

19.Air space is generally divided into two categories – regulated and unregulated. In regulated air space most of the traffic will be under a degree of control and special rules apply close to major airports, around military areas and along airway corridors. In Scotland the extent of control is much less than exists south of the Border, for the obvious reason that there is less air traffic and less congestion in air space. Apart from light–powered planes used for recreation, the other air sports, such as gliding, hang–gliding, para–gliding or ballooning, take place in unregulated air space.

ANNEX II: SUMMARY OF RECOMMENDED CHANGES TO LEGISLATION

1.There is already a wide range of powers to promote or regulate access for open–air recreation, many of which have had only limited use so far. Review of the legislation through commissioned studies and discussion with many authorities, as well as the subsequent general consultation, did not point to any major defects in existing statutory legislation. However, there were consistent views that the arrangements for rights of way need to be brought up to date and views were expressed that other elements of the Common Law on access (for example the use of force to remove people from land) do not match today's needs. As discussed elsewhere there were views on the need for a legal change to secure a right of access for open–air recreation.

2.It can be argued that the details of the arrangements for access agreements in Part II of the Countryside (Scotland) Act 1967 are cumbersome and in need of simplification; but there was no general call for such change. As noted earlier, these powers have been little used and it is feasible to use Management Agreements under Section 49A of the 1967 Act to achieve some (but not all) of the same ends.

3.This annex lists those areas where minor change or clarification to existing law would seem to be appropriate to meet changing needs, or to make an existing power more effective.

4.**Roads (Scotland) Act 1984:** Annex I (para 10) draws attention to the interaction between road traffic law and the common law on rights of way. Section 129(5) of the above Act makes it an offence to drive, ride, lead or propel a vehicle or a horse on a footpath, unless there is a right to do this. This is limiting on equestrians and cyclists given the hazards of the busy public road system. This interaction between roads law and the common law on rights of way should be examined.

5.**The terms footpath, public path etc:** The Roads (Scotland) Act 1984 defines a road as any way over which there is a public right of passage (Section 151(1)), a footpath being a way where the right is for pedestrian use.

6.The Countryside (Scotland) Act 1967 defines a public path as a footpath or a bridleway (Section 50(3)). These terms are further defined in Section 47 of the same Act, a footpath being a way over which the public have the following but no other right of way, that is to say, '... a right of way on foot with or without a right of way on pedal cycles'; and a bridleway is defined as '... a way over which the public have the following but no other rights of way, that is to say a right of way on foot and a right of way on horseback or leading a horse, with or without a right to drive animals of any description along that way'. The 1967 Act also uses the term 'public right of way' without definition. Simplification of this terminology is desirable.

7.**Assertion:** The term assertion, as used in the Countryside (Scotland) Act 1967 Section 46, is not clearly defined. At present, the extent of the duty laid on a planning authority is not clear. A simpler administrative system with clear procedures should resolve this matter.

8.**Public place:** A public place has the general definition of somewhere where the public have a right to be, but subsequent definition depends on interpretation, case by case. Commentators on the law relating to rights of way recognise that the interpretation of the term 'public place' causes difficulties because a right of way must begin and end at a public place. Lack of clarity arises where places to which the public resort regularly – a viewpoint or a natural feature such as a waterfall – may not be public places, being visited only through the tolerance of the owner, which may be withdrawn at any time. The Scottish Rights of Way Society suggests that a place of public resort should be a sufficient justification for the terminus of a right of way, but this would introduce a further definition which would require its own clarification

9.The definition of the term 'public place' should be examined with a view to it encompassing places regularly visited; or an alternative solution to the problem should be found, such as a right of way being required only to begin at a public place as presently defined.

DESIRABLE CHANGES TO THE LAW ON RIGHTS OF WAY LEGISLATION.

10.SNH does not believe that rights of way can meet all present-day access needs, but they do have an important place in a spectrum of approaches to improving access, especially on low ground and close to settlements.

11.The difficulties which authorities find in progressing rights of way work are well known and understandable. It is an area of work which is full of administrative difficulty, where progress is only made slowly and where, in difficult cases, there is a need to resort to the courts with all the potential costs involved. There are serious difficulties in assembling evidence for cases which might go to court and, at the end of the day, going to court can be an all–or–nothing process where loss of the case may put at risk any existing informal use of a route. In his assessment for the Access Review (SNH Review No 9), Professor Rowan–Robinson identified a number of key difficulties, and these are summarised under three heads.

–Because of the difficulties in making progress there has been a considerable loss of rights, particularly as a result of the increasing pace of change in the countryside, whether by land-use intensification for agriculture or forestry, or by built development, including new roads and motorways.

–Local authorities have a duty (under Section 46 of the Countryside (Scotland) Act 1967) to assert rights of way and various approaches to this have been adopted by different authorities. But unless the process is taken through the courts – a process sometimes called 'vindication' – and a declarator obtained to confirm the existence of the right, there is never any certainty. In other approaches to assertion – for example by confirmation by a Council of its belief in the existence of a right of way – the process is no more than establishing a forceful claim to which landowners may or may not accede.

–The third general problem is that there is a lack of finality in the process. In cases where a right of way has been agreed with owners and without proceeding as far as the courts, the matter is always open to be re-debated – say, by a new owner. Even where a declarator has been obtained through court action, this is never final, in that the rule of prescription still applies and any right so confirmed will lapse with 20 years of non–use.

12. The broad conclusion from review and the general public consultation must be that the present arrangements for the protection of rights of way are too weak, and that continued attrition is certain if no action is taken to change matters. There is a spiral of decline here: because the procedures are too complex, adequate record of rights of way does not exist, and because there is no adequate record, rights of way can be ignored where land management or development–led change occurs. The paucity of good records of rights of way precludes many people knowing about the existence of their rights and this in turn contributes to lack of use and, from lack of use, to routes falling into abeyance or being blocked, leading to eventual loss.

–The prime need is for a simplified administrative system allowing for the assertion of rights of way by local authorities, subject to objections by a procedure of written statement and a review by an independent reporter. There should be recourse to the law for procedural faults. Documentary evidence should be admissible in the process of assertion.

–Authorities should have a duty to prepare maps showing asserted rights of way and land to which the public has a right of access, either under access or footpath creation agreements (or orders) and other means of creating formal rights of access by the public, such as might be agreed as a condition of Capital Tax exemptions. Authorities might also wish to use these maps to document other permissive or agreed routes but distinguishing clearly that these do not have right of way status. Section 26 of the Countryside (Scotland) Act 1967 requires Councils to keep maps of access agreement areas and an amendment to widen this duty would be an appropriate way of achieving this end.

–The basic criteria for a right of way should be restated, first to make clear that the concept of 'tolerance of use' should be set aside in favour of 'open and freely used'. Second, the end point criteria for a right of way should be re–examined (see para 8).

–The status of a right of way, once asserted, should be secure until evidence is brought forward (under the new administrative procedure mentioned above) to prove its non–use over the prescriptive period.

–Although not thought to be in doubt, recreational use of rights of way should be confirmed in statute.

–Public bodies involved in land management or development should have a general duty to secure that in their operations they have regard to the legitimate needs of the public to have access to the countryside for open–air recreation including the protection of rights of way.

–The existing statutory restraint on pasturing bulls on land crossed by a right of way (Section 44 of the Countryside (Scotland) Act 1967) is now out of date and should be amended to refer to the keeping of any animal known to be dangerous to the public.

–Local authorities should have a duty to maintain rights of way which have been fully asserted under the new administrative system, but only to a standard appropriate to their location and levels of use.

–Strengthened powers to the local Councils to manage footpaths and rights of way are needed, in particular:

powers to remove an obstruction (including misleading signs) and to recover costs for removing obstructions which are deliberate or malicious;

a duty to signpost asserted rights of way and powers to waymark and otherwise promote walking opportunities in a Council's area;

a range of powers to enable management and maintenance should be confirmed; in particular, authorities should be able to:

> works to safeguard or maintain any right of way, to bring in materials or equipment for this purpose by the most convenient route and to use local materials from borrow–pits (with restoration of vegetation cover), all subject to consultation with owners;

> to construct a bridge or to adopt any bridge or related structure which is unsafe and to take appropriate action to secure safe passage by the public;

> to erect gates, stiles or fences; and

> to give consent to other organisations to undertake approved programmes of management and maintenance.

These management powers should apply to land subject to Access and Public Path Creation Agreements and Orders.

–For rights of way there should be offences for:

deliberately blocking or otherwise impeding the use of a right of way; and

erecting misleading signs.

ACCESS TO OPEN COUNTRY

13.In Chapter 3 it was concluded that it is unsatisfactory for someone exercising the customary liberty to be on open country for the purposes of peaceful open–air recreation to be a trespasser, (unless there by consent, on a right of way or where access has been specially negotiated). In this circumstance visitors have no clarity about their status and will always be uncertain as to whether they have any sanction to be where they are. SNH concludes that there should be no change in the general law at present, preferring to seek to work for improved access through negotiation and tolerance, but it wishes to stimulate discussion on removing the 'stigma' of the peaceful visitor being a trespasser when on open country.

14.SNH believes that a person taking access for peaceful open-air recreation over open country should not be regarded in law as a trespasser unless required to leave by a proprietor or someone acting with his authority. SNH would hope that landowners will exercise their right to ask people to leave with discretion and only with good cause. A proprietor or his agent would not be deprived of their right to require a person enjoying access on the terms above to leave. Nor would a change on these lines affect a proprietor's right to constrain entry by a named individual through interdict, nor should it create any burden on the land.

15.The definition of open country should be as used in the Countryside (Scotland) Act 1967, namely: '... any land appearing to SNH or the authority ... to consist wholly or predominately of mountain, moor, heath, hill, woodland, cliff or foreshore, and any waterway; and in this section 'waterway' and 'foreshore' shall include any bank, barrier, dune, beach, flat or other land adjacent to the waterway or foreshore'. A legislative change of this kind would essentially confirm the status quo of existing use of open country by the public. It would have the clear advantage of giving the public a much greater sense of security that they can be on some categories of land or on water for peaceful open–air recreation without fear of being in the wrong.

16.Lastly, there should be review of the use of 'reasonable force'. In Chapter 3 it is argued that the use of force should no longer be regarded as an appropriate remedy for a civil wrong.

ANNEX III: REVIEW OF THE ISSUES INVOLVED IN CREATING A LEGAL RIGHT OF ACCESS TO LAND

INTRODUCTION

1.Debate about rights of access to land in Scotland has a deep cultural and historical context which predates contemporary interest in recreational access and which has strong political resonances to this day. The recreational claim to access, by a mainly urban public, began in the last century; it reached Parliament in the unsuccessful attempts, led by James Bryce MP, to promote an Access to the Mountains Bill around 100 years ago. Parliamentary interest on the subject has continued up to the present, with a Freedom to Roam Bill presented this year (1994) by Mrs Margaret Ewing MP.

2.As part of wartime debate about improved arrangements for enjoyment of the countryside, the Hobhouse Committee (in reviewing proposals for National Parks in England and Wales, 1947) recommended that there should be a right of access for recreation to open country. To the disappointment of recreation interests, the reforming post–war Government did not act on this recommendation but brought in powers in the National Parks and Access to the Countryside Act 1949 for local authorities (south of the Border) to enter into Access Agreements with owners. These same access powers were adopted directly into the Countryside (Scotland) Act 1967 but, as described in Chapter 3, they have had little use.

3.Debate on this matter has continued south of the Border in recent discussions about new legislation for common land, and also in the Edwards Committee Review of National Parks *Fit for the Future* (1991) which stopped short of recommending an unqualified right of access in favour of negotiations and other action to secure a presumption of open access, but subject to a safeguard for land owners that they should be able to argue the case why this should not apply to their land.

4.In Chapter 3, SNH concluded that the best way forward is to seek to improve present arrangements for access to open country through the voluntary principle. However, SNH also argues that the legal position should be brought into line with present–day practice by rectifying the technicality whereby a person on open country for peaceful open-air recreation is strictly a trespasser. This Annex develops the reasons set out in Chapter 3 as to why SNH thinks that a more radical change to the law should not be made at present.

DIFFICULTIES IN ACCESS TO OPEN COUNTRY

5.Present–day use of the higher hills for recreation is mainly unrestrained although there are places where difficulties are experienced. It is claimed that these difficulties are more prevalent for the smaller blocks of open land, particularly where the visitor has first to pass through enclosed farm land and where routes for this are neither obvious nor welcoming. There is, however, a widespread perception among the recreation interests that there are now more impediments to access, more restrictive signs and more threat to the customary use of hill land for recreation. Equally, land owners and managers express concern that numbers of visitors continue to increase, with more impact on their management activities.

6. There is a major imbalance in debate about access to open country, in that most concern focuses on the higher hills compared with more local open land and, most especially, to the open coast, which is of greater recreational importance to a much larger number of people. Visits to the coast greatly exceed numbers of people going to the mountains, but few responses to the Consultation Paper referred to this.

7. In a practical sense, access to the higher hills does not raise major difficulties for the visitor. But there can be poor accessibility to open country, especially to some smaller areas of open country, including the coast, and access in some places is still unwelcoming. Opinions on the matter can be strongly held, ranging from a desire to feel entirely free to enjoy open spaces, to more uncompromising views on tenure and land use. The political issues which underlie this debate are a matter for resolution through the democratic process: the practical needs for public access should, in the first instance, be addressed in other ways.

8. A change in the law to create a right of access for recreation would impinge on rights in property. Proponents of a right of access are generally agreed that there would need to be restraints to protect reasonable privacy and the operational needs of land management and to promote good behaviour. Formalising access could raise other issues of where, how and for what purpose the right might be exercised, as discussed below. None of these issues is irresolvable, but they would involve consideration of matters which are at present left mainly to discretion.

THE SCOPE OF A RIGHT TO OPEN–AIR RECREATION

9. **Definition:** There is no definition in any statute of the words 'enjoyment' or 'open–air recreation', except that the National Parks and Access to the Countryside Act 1949 (as it applies to England and Wales) excludes organised games. It is not easy to categorise recreation along a spectrum from informal to formal or from passive to active, and existing use of open country covers a very wide range of pastimes and pursuits, some dependent on the qualities of the place in which they are enjoyed, others using the outdoors as a venue or arena for the activity. Recreations have diversified greatly in the past two decades, some of them being now highly dependent on sophisticated equipment. So defining the limits of recreation raises some questions.

10. **Territorial extent:** While some people think that there should be a general right of access to land (subject to safeguards) most people who want a change in the law are concerned about access

over hill land. If a change were to do more than simply legitimise what experienced hill-goers enjoy already, any right of access would have to address difficulties at the interface between open and fenced farmland and also secure access to the coast. Defining territorial limits to a right of access would not be easy.

11.**Who would benefit?** Most recreation is by individuals or by people in small groups of friends or family. There is, however, increasing use of land or water for enjoyment by organised groups, sometimes as clubs, sometimes as training or guided groups. There is more use of the countryside for educational purposes, from parties visiting land for formal training and education through to holiday groups, some of which have a charitable or voluntary body leadership, others being fully commercial.

12.**Ancillary activities:** There is a range of activities ancillary to recreation which people practise by custom and tolerance. The gathering of natural fruits is normally a harmless, enjoyable pursuit, although there is evidence of increasing commercial gathering of natural products on private land, for example mushrooms and shellfish. Lighting fires and camping on private land are activities which are adjuncts to enjoyment of the outdoors but, in law, both are strictly an offence under the Trespass (Scotland) Act 1867. When done with care and on an individual basis, little harm is done by camping in the countryside. The lighting of fires tends to have more impact, both in damage to the ground and from collection of firewood from nearby trees, and it can cause serious and widespread damage to land if allowed to get out of control.

13.**Temporal limitations:** The operational needs of land management and of conservation might raise questions about temporal limitations to access. A balance would have to be struck on temporal limitations, as any restraints of this kind which were perceived to be unreasonable would be at risk of being disregarded and unenforceable: thus, comprehensive restrictions over the whole shooting and stalking period would not be enforceable. Some restrictions might also be justified on conservation grounds, either as general restraint on visiting a location of historic or natural value, or temporal, to protect plants and animals from disturbance at critical periods in their development. Again, enforcement of any restraints of this kind would require (for extensive areas of open country) that the limitations are not just seen to be valid by their proposers but are acceptable to, and adopted by, the recreational interests.

14.**Behaviour:** The criminal law already bears on many aspects of how people behave when on land and the new Criminal Justice and Public Order Act adds significantly to general restraint on the behaviour of people when on land. The powers for Access Agreements list (Schedule 2 of the 1967 Countryside (Scotland) Act) a set of standard prohibitions on what people may do when on land covered by an Agreement. There is nothing in these eleven limitations (which range from driving or riding a vehicle to anything to anything which wantonly disturbs, annoys or obstructs any person engaged in any lawful occupation) which is unreasonable but the list reads like a set of park by–laws and issues of enforcement and compliance govern the reality of using such powers.

15.**Privacy:** An important safeguard for those who live and work in the countryside would be reasonable protection of their privacy. Clearly it would be proper to exclude access to properties and their curtilage – although the latter can be difficult to define. A distance qualification might provide one approach but that would be awkward where a long–standing access route already passes close to or through a property. Having special rules for privacy for rural dwellers might be thought preferential in relation to towns and cities where adverse effects on property are much more likely.

THE APPLICATION OF A RIGHT OF ACCESS

16.A right of access would raise a number of practical issues in its application. There are general issues of equity involved, in that a change in the law should not affect rights in property to the point where an owner's enjoyment or management are significantly impaired: a fair balance has to be struck between public and private interests in taking access to land. Striking this balance is not just a matter for the law; it must involve consideration and good sense.

17.**Liability:** Land-owners have liability to people on their land which founds on the common law duty of care, as formalised through statute law (the Occupiers Liability Act) and Health and Safety Regulations. The way in which people make use of natural resources for outdoor recreation – especially for activities with inherent hazard – may place them well beyond any duty of care from the landowner. It is asserted by those involved in active sports that the principle of *volente non fit injuria* (a willing person cannot be injured) removes any obligation from the land owner or manager, but this is a limited defence which does not absolve participants in recreation of their duty of care in relation to an owner's interest or indeed to fellow participants. The matter of liability in active pursuits is full of uncertainty, in part because of the novel and sometimes extreme circumstances which can arise, and there is a trend for people to become more litigious.

18.If there were to be a major change in the legal basis of access, then this could impinge on public liability. For example, there might be a strengthened duty of care for the visitor in relation to any obligations to act responsibly, and some land owners and managers might carry a broader duty by virtue of their knowing that people were now able to be on their land legally rather than as previously in a (normally) uninvited status. All parties might become more concerned to guard their interests.

19.**Accessibility:** Some owners might wish to restrain entry to their land or to maintain closer supervision of it by reducing accessibility. This might involve closing off or fencing some access points or informal car parks. Land which is at present open and perhaps visited by the public might be fenced or put to some other kind of management – for example grazing or tree planting – with the covert purpose of reducing accessibility. There is some evidence that this occurs already, although there are remedies in that local authorities have the powers to undertake management and to provide facilities in order to enhance accessibility. A formal power on access could lead to more guarding of property by reducing the present levels of accessibility.

20.**Enforcement of limitations:** The main options for enforcing limitations are that breach of them become a criminal offence or that they come under civil law. Byelaw powers might be usable in some circumstances. The criminal offence option would certainly be regarded as overbearing for minor transgressions to the rules, but the civil law route would leave the land owner and manager with only limited ability to protect their interests because the difficulties of enforcement could be formidable. The police in all likelihood would be anxious not to become involved in this type of dispute between individuals. The practicality of chasing and identifying, say, a hill-walker on a ridge or a canoeist on a river would make the process of identification or gathering evidence virtually impossible. The introduction of new law which would have a likelihood from the outset of being disregarded or which could not be effectively enforced is not to be considered lightly.

DISCUSSION

21.The above analysis of the issues involved in a change in the law to provide for free access to land does not suggest that such a change would be impossible: with determination the technical difficulties could no doubt be overcome. It would, however, be difficult to achieve in practice the right balance between the interests of land owners and public recreation. If these matters were not addressed directly in statute and left to evolving practice and the courts to determine, this would itself cause uncertainty.

22.Other countries – especially in Scandinavia – have statutory (or common law equivalent) arrangements for access which operate reasonably well, and these models are often cited in debate about access, especially as Highland Scotland provides a physical analogue at a smaller scale to the Nordic countries.

23.However, comparison with the Nordic countries must be tempered by some caution. First, there is the much greater extent of available open country compared with small populations – Norway, Sweden and Finland are the least densely populated countries in mainland Europe. Second, the populations of these countries have a closer cultural involvement in and respect for the outdoors than now exists in urban Britain, and the right of generally free access has been carried through from a previously all–rural economy.

24.The existence of a right of access does not preclude the need for local management of it or for local restraint and, increasingly, more management and restrictions are needed close to cities, in the busy tourist areas and in the National Parks. In addition, the right of access in these countries is viewed by local people as part of their cultural inheritance. Its exercise by large numbers of visitors can lead to some attrition to the welcome they receive.

25.In assessing the issues debated in the paragraphs above, SNH comes to the conclusion that introduction of a legal right of access is not impossible, but that it does raise more complex issues than are generally accepted by the proponents of change of this kind. The framing of any law of this kind would require care lest anything omitted be deemed to be outwith the general right.

26.The net effect of formalising the basis of access might well be to make land mangers and visitors alike more jealous of their rights and more vigilant in their guarding of obligations and, in this way, might increase friction rather than reduce it. The ability of a land owner or manager to protect their legitimate operational needs would be limited unless additional and probably unworkable sanctions under the criminal law were to be enacted. Codification of the law in this way may ultimately prove necessary; SNH does not, however, regard it as clearly preferable to arrangements based on tolerance, goodwill and mutual respect, so long as this works successfully. In SNH's judgement the circumstances currently exist to improve access on this basis and for this reason it has decided that a substantive change to the law is not desirable at present.

ANNEX IV: RESEARCH PROJECTS UNDERTAKEN FOR THE REVIEW

In the initial stages of the Review the former Countryside Commission for Scotland set in hand a major programme of fact–finding to help inform the policy debate. While some of this work was undertaken in–house, most of it was contracted to consultants, as listed below. There are many gaps still in our understanding of how the countryside is used for open–air recreation but the projects listed below comprise the most substantial programme of survey undertaken on access to the Scottish countryside for open-air recreation. All the research material is on open access and most of it has been published. Details of availability are given below for each project.

–A survey of the involvement of planning authorities on work on public rights of way and other footpaths. A questionnaire survey of 43 planning authorities was carried out in conjunction with the CCS/COSLA Working Party on Footpaths and Walks for Recreation. Some 40 authorities responded to the questionnaire.

Typescript report available from Recreation and Access Branch (address below).

–A survey of walking in the countryside. Some 4,000 people were interviewed across Scotland in April, July, October (1990) and January (1991) in the Scottish Opinion Survey run by System Three Scotland. Information on walkers and non–walkers, and on the characteristics of walks undertaken, was collected.

SNH Research Survey and Monitoring Report No 3 £5.00

–A survey of public attitudes to walking and access issues. Over 1,000 people were interviewed across Scotland in February 1991 as part of the Scottish Opinion Survey run by System Three Scotland and asked questions on their concerns about and attitudes to the use of the countryside for open–air recreation.

SNH Research Survey and Monitoring Report No 4 £5.00.

–Footpaths and access in Scotland's countryside. This study, undertaken by Peter Scott Planning Services, examined how access is working at the local level in Scotland. Eight areas around Scotland were studied (the Angus coast, Balquhidder/Strathyre, Bathgate hills, East Lothian/Haddington, Paisley/Neilston, Oban/Benderloch, River Tweed and Glen Torridon/Glen Carron). The extent and condition of the network of access routes in these study areas were assessed, and in–depth interviews were undertaken with 102 people representing some 113 landowners, farmers and community, recreation and conservation organisations.

SNH Research Survey and Monitoring Report No 2. £7.50

An 18 page summary is available Free.

–**Review of rights of way procedures.** This review, undertaken by Professor Rowan–Robinson of the University of Aberdeen, involved the preparation of statements of the statute and common law (by Colin Reid of the University of Dundee Law Department and Professor Bill Gordon of the University of Glasgow Law Department respectively). Interviews were held with 17 planning authorities and 14 other organisations representing landowners, farmers and recreation groups, and current practice was reviewed. Proposals for reform to practice and procedure were put forward and a guide to the law and its use prepared.

SNH Review No 9   £5.00

Public Access to the Countryside: *A Guide to the Law Practice and Procedure in Scotland. 1993.* SNH in association with COSLA.
£7.50

–**The law of access for water–based recreation.** This review was undertaken by Brodies WS, a firm of solicitors in Edinburgh. A comprehensive statement on the law of access to and on water and its application was prepared. Some 20 groups and organisations were interviewed, including all those with a central interest in the subject, and submissions were received from 40 planning authorities and 48 other organisations.

Available for inspection.

–**Economics of countryside access in Scotland.** This study considered the economic factors involved in countryside recreation, and was undertaken by the Scottish Agricultural College, Aberdeen. The study assessed the overall economic value of open-air recreation in Scotland, and examined the costs and benefits arising at the level of the land management unit (farm or estate). Data were gathered through a postal survey of 1,200 farms and estates, and detailed interviews with 50 owners or occupiers.

Scottish Agricultural College Economics Report No 37 1992.
£15.00

–**Countryside access in Europe.** Peter Scott Planning Services was commissioned to review access arrangements in Austria, Denmark, France, Germany, the Netherlands, Norway, Sweden and Switzerland. The country reviews were sub–contracted to consultants with specialist knowledge of each country and an overview prepared by the main consultant. The study considered access arrangements and traditions, legislation, management and their strengths and weaknesses.

SNH Review Series No 23   £5.00

–Survey of farmers' attitudes to access. With funding mainly from the Countryside Commission for Scotland and with a contribution from Central Region, FWAG undertook an in–depth interview survey of attitudes to conservation held by a sample of 100 farmers in Central Region. Questions on respondents' attitudes towards access were included and these were presented in a separate report.

Available for inspection.

–Organised activities and training in the countryside. This study, undertaken by Drennan Watson of Landwise, assessed the extent of the use of the countryside by organised training and educational groups, and issues arising therefrom.

Available for inspection.

–Review of local authority expenditure on open–air recreation. Peter Scott Planning Services was commissioned to review local authority and other public sector expenditure on providing for and managing access and open–air recreation. Data were gathered by a questionnaire survey to local authorities on relevant expenditure in the financial year 1990/91, and a broader perspective was gained by examination of local authority financial returns for previous years.

Available for inspection.

SNH reports are available from:

Publications Section
Scottish Natural Heritage
Battleby
Redgorton
Perth PH1 3EW
tel: 01738 627921

Prices quoted include postage. Gratis items can be obtained from the Publications Section and at most main SNH offices (address in your local telephone book) or from Recreation and Access Branch, Scottish Natural Heritage, 2 Anderson Place, EdinburghEH6 5NP (Tel 0131 446 2468).

Reports which are available for inspection can be seen at main SNH offices (for Edinburgh, at Recreation and Access Branch, address above). In all cases please phone in advance.

ANNEX V: PUBLIC CONSULTATION

1.In the early stages of the review, the Countryside Commission for Scotland undertook a substantial programme of data gathering through the research listed in Annex IV and also from contact with many of the organisations involved in recreation in the countryside. A Technical Advisory Group provided a Forum for discussion of some of the key issues and of the research programme. These initial contacts did not add up to a comprehensive consultation of all interested parties, so a general consultation was launched by SNH in January 1993.

2.Some 14,000 copies of a discussion paper Enjoying the Outdoors were distributed to national organisations with an involvement or interest in open–air recreation; to the local authorities; and to many local interest groups such as community groups, land management interests and local recreation organisations. Rural Forum circulated the paper to Community Councils and an effort was made to reach the general public through general press publicity, and circulation of copies of the report to all public libraries in Scotland.

3.Almost 500 responses were received. These came mainly from public bodies, recreation interest groups and land owners, but 169 responses were received from private individuals. The content of these responses was wide ranging: many of the individual responses were long and detailed, reflecting the keen interest which the subject of access can arouse. The submissions provided SNH with a valuable archive of opinions, observations and ideas on access matters which have contributed to its thinking.

4.Apart from six respondents who requested confidentiality, the responses are on the open record and may be seen at SNH's Recreation and Access Branch, 2 Anderson Place, Edinburgh EH6 5NP. Anyone wishing to see the responses should make an appointment in advance (telephone 0131–4462468).

5.SNH commissioned Tourism and Rural Initiatives Consultancy Ltd – a consultancy based in Fife – to prepare an overview of these responses. This independent review was undertaken in the interests of objectivity. A summary report from this review has been published and circulated to all respondents. A list of respondents is provided in the summary: Enjoying the Outdoors – a Summary Report of Responses to the Consultation Paper. Copies of the summary report are available gratis on request to Publications Section, Scottish Natural Heritage, Battleby, Redgorton, Perth PH1 3EW, (01738 627921) or from Recreation and Access Branch (address as above) or main SNH offices (address in your local telephone book).